WHEN LIFE GETS TOUGH

WHEN LIFE GETS TOUGH

TRIXIE JELLIE

When Life Gets Tough
Published by Trixie Jellie
New Zealand

ISBN 978-0-473-40999-9 (Softcover)
ISBN 978-0-473-41000-1 (ePUB)
ISBN 978-0-473-41001-8 (Kindle)

Editing:
Andrew Killick & Andrea Candy

Production & Typesetting:
Andrew Killick
Castle Publishing Services
www.castlepublishing.co.nz

Cover design:
Paul Smith

Author photo:
Mark Scowen
www.intense.co.nz

To my husband Howard.

You have stood with me through these trials, with your love, encouragement and godly wisdom. You are a man of integrity – thank you for being you. I love you, we are one.

Forewords

How would you react if someone tried to kill you by flinging you off a bridge? How would an experience like that impact your faith and your attitudes about life?

I was shocked by the story when I saw it on the front page of the *New Zealand Herald.* It was national news – Trixie Jellie, an ordinary woman innocently going about her errands, had found herself in the worst kind of situation. I didn't know Trixie personally, but my heart went out to her and I started to pray. Her injuries from this terrible assault by a total stranger were horrific and life-threatening.

Some time later, I met Trixie face to face, and it soon became clear that she was a woman of great faith. Today, I count her among my dearest friends, and I encouraged her to write this book to tell people about her challenges – not only the episode at the bridge but many other things as well. We can all learn from, and be inspired by, her experiences.

Trixie has led a truly inspirational life. It is simply amazing how she has recovered physically, mentally and spiritually, with forgiveness being one of the keys to being able to achieve this.

She has victoriously walked through so many difficulties. As she tells her story, you will be able to feel her heartbeat, and be spurred on by her determination, her extraordinary courage and her faith.

When Life Gets Tough is sometimes a heart-rending read, but it also contains an amazing amount of positivity and joy. It includes many examples of Trixie's encounters with the people she meets, and how she has reached out to them in love.

Our lives may not be as dramatic as Trixie's, but they can be an exciting walk by faith every day, no matter what situations come our way. I encourage you to read, and be inspired by, this book – then hand it on to others – so that when life gets tough we can know that God is with us through it all.

Di Willis, Dip OT, QSM
Ministries Director, Elevate Christian Disability Trust

❧

At City Impact Church, we have had the privilege of 'doing life' together with Trixie and I feel even more privileged now to have read her story through her eyes.

Her real and transparent account attest to a woman of God who has a very real relationship with her Saviour, Jesus Christ. Trixie is a woman who has shown character and courage in the face of adversity, along with a tenacious 'grit', standing on God's promises.

This is an easy-to-read story that will entertain, inspire and encourage as it reveals the source of the grace, peace and joy she has managed to find in the midst of the storms.

I trust that as you share in her story, you too will share the Source of the love and courage she has experienced…

Kim Burger, BPsych, Dip Counselling
Pastor and Elder, City Impact Church, Auckland

❧

Having known Trixie and her family for over 16 years, it is with great pleasure that I write this foreword for her book, *When Life Gets Tough.*

Trixie has been a woman of faith, determination and perseverance who has overcome some incredible challenges in her life.

While we all have a story to tell and all face challenges – I hope not quite as monumental as Trixie's testimony reveals – it is encouraging to hear her story and how her faith in Christ has empowered her to be the woman she is today.

Being planted in church, reading the Bible and being a woman of prayer have equipped Trixie to work through the hurts, the disappointments, the challenges that come to us all, with love, grace and forgiveness – and still be smiling.

I encourage you to read her story as it is stories like hers that help us all to move on with the right attitude and character.

I commend Trixie for putting pen to paper – for being so honest and vulnerable in sharing her story in a way that not only glorifies her Lord and Saviour but will also bring encouragement to you, the reader.

I know that is her prayer and the motive for this well-written, easy-reading, true life story.

Pastor Peter Mortlock
Senior Pastor, City Impact Churches International

Acknowledgements

To Hugh and Di Willis, without whose encouragement, support and hard work, this book would not have been written. I will be forever be in your debt.

To my daughter Allison, who gave up her time so freely, had unlimited patience developing my computer skills, and assisted with the development of this book.

To my son Trevor, for his unwavering support and guidance.

To Jean Clark, for her prayers, wise counsel and friendship. Thank you for being my mentor.

To Yvonne Bindon for her expertise in proofreading my journey and being my friend for all these many years.

To Castle Publishing, a big thank you for your patient endurance over the last few years. A great team to work with.

To all those public servants, police, hospital nurses and doctors, specialists and ACC case managers who helped me in my recovery over many years. We are very fortunate to live in this country with its wonderful support services.

To Forrest Hill Presbyterian Church, your support was amazing.

To my Christian family at City Impact Church, for their love and fellowship, and the teaching I have received in this wonderful Christian community.

Contents

Preface

In 1987, while I was talking to God as I did my housework – dishes, making the beds, the usual things we mums do – God spoke to me and said, "I want you to keep a record of everything I will do in your life as it happens." I had never kept a journal but I did from that day on.

About two years later, on 21 April 1989, I was attacked and thrown off the Myers Park overbridge in Auckland. Six weeks into my recuperation, the staff at the Auckland Airport catering company where my husband Howard worked, took up a collection for me. Amongst other things, the money was used to buy a cassette player which enabled me to make an audio recording of my life's journey as I lay in my hospital bed. Writing while lying on my back was not easy so I was very grateful for this gift.

In 2000, Howard and I were travelling around Golden Bay in the upper South Island of New Zealand when God spoke to me again. He said, "I want you to write a book." I think I gasped. When I told Howard, he looked at me with surprise and said, "What?" I repeated what God had said. Howard didn't say anything – I think he was thinking the same as me. I was busy telling God, "I don't know how to write a book." I found it difficult to write a letter let alone a book! I only started reading books when I was married.

As the years have gone by, I have had many people say to me, "You need to write a book," or "When are you going to write a book?" In March 2015, Pastor John Bevere came to our church,

City Impact, and told us the story of how God asked him to write a book. Like me, he had also said to God, "But I don't know how to write a book!" At school he had lower English grades than anyone else he had ever spoken to – he just didn't feel qualified. Later, two women came up to him at separate conferences in different parts of the USA and gave him a very similar message. One woman said God had told her to tell Pastor John that he was to write a book; the second said, "God said if you don't write the book, He will find someone else!"

Pastor John went home and said to the Holy Spirit, who is God living within His children, "I don't know how to do this, but I believe you will help me." The rest was history, he told us. "I have now written 19 books which have gone around the world and been translated into different languages. Some have become best sellers."

This really got my attention and spoke volumes to me. I walked out of the service and got a wonderful hug from my friend Di. I told her how the message had made me sit up and think that maybe I could do what God had been asking me to do. I added, "I just simply don't know where to start."

"Just make a start," she replied, "then send it to Hugh and me, and we will help you. We have helped others to write books."

I went home believing God had sent the right people to me. I had a sense of reassurance that this was the right time and that everything would fall into place. I sat at the computer after committing this huge project to Jesus and asked the Holy Spirit to guide me – it would be His book, not mine. The story just flowed. When I had completed 26 pages, I sent them to Di's husband Hugh, saying, "This is only to get your opinion as to whether it's worthwhile carrying on the way I have started." Hugh rang the next day to ask me to send the working document to him so he could start making it more readable and improve my grammar. Wow! How do you think I slept after that? But here we are, and it is only by the grace of God that I have been able to do this, with the help of my dear friends, Hugh and Di Willis.

I pray that this book will help all who read it to see that our God is interested in even the smallest things in our lives, not just the big events. God wants us to have an intimate relationship with Him. He knows everything about us and we need to get to know Him. The closer we get, the more we learn that nothing is impossible for Him.

Let me say here that this act of attempted murder on my life was horrifying to my family and those who know me personally. If you are looking for a book that will grip you with the horror of what took place, you will be disappointed. I am not able to explain the horror because I did not experience it. Jesus protected me from it all. I had no bad memories, bad dreams, flashbacks or pain. My purpose in writing this book is to speak into the lives of many people who struggle with the terrible things that have happened or are happening in their lives and who wonder how they will ever cope. God has created us to be strong in adversity, and with His help and strength we will get through.

This is my story, my journey. I pray it will speak to you of how much God loves you and wants the best for you and your family.

PART ONE

From Out of Nowhere

CHAPTER ONE

Attempted Murder

"It's in the paper this morning, Mum; they have apprehended the man who tried to murder you."

"Murder! What do you mean *murder*?" I was talking to my son Trevor while lying in my hospital bed in Ward 8 at Auckland Hospital on a Monday morning when he made this statement to me.

He repeated himself, trying to get me to understand. "Mum, it was in the paper this morning. When you were thrown off the bridge, it was *attempted murder*." The information took a while to sink in, then it suddenly dawned on me that being attacked, beaten up and thrown off a bridge in central Auckland at 9:30 in the morning was indeed 'attempted murder', and that Trevor and the newspaper really were talking about *me*.

At this time in my life I was a 42-year-old wife and mother of three beautiful children: Chris (18), Trevor (16) and Allison (8). This is how it happened…

On an ordinary Friday morning in 1989 I took my mum to get her passport renewed. As we drove into Auckland City, always happy in each other's company, I turned onto Mayoral Drive and found a car park on the Myers Park bridge which most people know as the Mayoral Drive overbridge. It is just behind the Auckland Town Hall with a car park underneath. Having finished our business at the passport office, we walked back to my car. The day was perfect and as I pointed out the beautiful trees in autumn colour and a helicopter reflected in the windows of a blue-glass building, everything was peaceful in our world. As we approached my car I noticed a young man leaning on the handrail of the overbridge. When we drew closer he stepped out in front of us and, gesturing to the vehicles parked under the bridge, asked if we knew who owned the blue car below?

As I looked over the side I heard a quiet voice within say to me, "You are going over the bridge." Responding immediately, I grabbed Mum, who had not heard what the man said. She was hard of hearing and asked, "What did he say, dear?" Fortunately my car was right beside us. I managed to open the door and literally stuff her in, locking the door.

The man, whose name was Richard, was 19 years old. He took me in a headlock and started to beat me, dragging me towards the railing of the bridge. I have always believed there is good and evil in this world and evil was what I was facing right now. I spoke out, "Get behind me, Satan!" Eventually I was on top of the handrail with my left leg through the bars trying to stop myself from going over. As I fell I cried, "Jesus, save me."

Workers in the building next to the bridge heard me scream as I fell. With a thud, I landed on top of a car and slid off the back. I must have hit my forehead on the tow bar, as I had a big dent that required numerous stitches, although fortunately my skull was not cracked. I don't remember what happened next, but Jesus had answered my prayer and I was alive.

I was told later by the police I was still conscious. The constable who came to my aid said I was able to speak and tell him what had happened and give him my details. Another police officer apprehended Richard. As it happens, Auckland's Central Police Station is just up the road from where I was attacked. These two officers were returning from fitness training and had stopped at the traffic lights nearby so were right on hand to help me.

It transpired that Richard had thought about throwing an elderly couple off the overbridge but had seen us coming so waited for me. He was a student at the Auckland University of Technology (AUT) but had been so agitated that morning, he was told to go for counselling. When they couldn't see him straightaway, he went back to class, slammed his books shut, said, "Stuff the lot of you," then came down to the bridge, believing God had told him to kill someone that day.

During the attack, Mum had tried to open the car door but couldn't. After I had gone over the side she managed to attract a man's attention by saying, "That's my daughter." He then helped her get out of the car and she looked over the side to see me motionless on the ground below.

The immediate aftermath

After I had been taken away in the ambulance the police took Mum to the police station and asked her to ring Howard. His secretary said he was in a meeting and could not be interrupted. Mum told her who she was and that his wife had had a terrible accident. Howard's secretary brought him to the phone and Mum had the awful job of telling him what had happened.

Howard also filled in some details for me. He was at work at the airport, where he was manager of catering at the time. He left there and came to see me at the hospital. My eyes locked onto him the minute he walked into the emergency department and he held my hand while the medical staff put me on life support. From there he had to go to see to our children while I went into theatre for a five-hour operation. The doctor told him to go home as I would not be conscious until early the next morning.

Unfortunately my name was aired on the 2 p.m. news bulletin

before my family was told what had happened. It caused a lot of mayhem – friends fainted, some people did very silly things while driving, one person's car door was ripped off while they were reversing, another car ended up in a ditch. When my sister-in-law Joan heard of it, she immediately rushed to the hospital and sat outside my room praying. Howard picked up our 8-year-old daughter Allison from school. He told her that Mummy had had an accident and was in hospital. He then went to Westlake Boys High School to collect Trevor – the school had already heard the news and recommended he wait until his father came. When they arrived home, Howard rang Manukau Tech to ask them to stop Chris from driving home. They found him about to get into his car and organised someone to give him a lift. Hearing about it on the radio while driving would have meant disaster. I can only imagine the pain my dear family went through that night, having been told I might not make it.

Early next morning, Saturday, Howard came back to the hospital and waited until I awoke. I remember thinking, "Goodness! That was a very weird dream." I opened the one eye I could see out of, which was only a slit, and soon realised it was no dream. There was my beloved Howard looking at me with concern. I was on life support, unable to speak to him, and had extensive injuries. My pelvis was smashed like cornflakes. I had five breaks from my left hip down to the knee with a plate and screws holding it together. My forehead had a huge dent with a lot of stitches. I lost finger nails on my left hand and I had a metal rod put through my left leg to hold nine pounds of weight to stop that leg becoming shorter than the right. Dr Stan explained I would spend the next ten weeks flat on my back as it would take that length of time for my bones to heal. He said I could not use a pillow or I would always have a bent back.

When Howard could see I was going to be okay, he left for home.

He made arrangements for Allison to go to her friend's place as he thought it would be better for her to see me in a day or two when I was off life support. He also thought it best not to tell Allison the details of what had happened to me. Her little friends where she had gone to play knew and they asked her, "What did your mummy look like after being thrown off a bridge?" Allison was so shocked by what she heard she ran home by herself to talk to her daddy about it, only to find her daddy and one of her brothers in each other's arms, crying. The realisation that it was true really hit home then. Unfortunately she didn't tell them she was there. Instead, she went to her room and cried by herself.

Howard brought the boys over to see me later in the morning. Chris was oozing anger. I made as though I wanted to write something and my sister Airdre laid a pad and pen on my tummy. I couldn't see what I was doing but I wrote, "Chris, you must forgive him." The leaders of the Bible in Schools training programme I had been doing also visited me. They were concerned that I needed to forgive my attacker and read me the Bible story about Joseph forgiving his brothers for selling him into slavery. Before they could finish their story, I had written on my pad, "Already forgiven."

My wonderful doctor Stan, who used to call me his 'miracle lady', came in a few times throughout the day. I asked him for a steak sandwich (in writing of course) as I wanted to be off the feeding tube and was sure I could handle it. He told me that if I felt like that the following morning, he would think about it. On Sunday I was taken off life support although the feeding tube through my nose stayed in, with the nurses saying, "We'll see how you are later in the day." The next time I was given a liquid meal through the feeding tube, I threw it straight back up. After this, the nurse removed the tube and I never looked back.

Now that I was connected to fewer tubes, Howard decided to bring Allison in for a visit. I remember the look in her eyes as she saw me for the first time. Howard carried her to me and said, "Why don't you give Mummy a kiss?" Later she told me that she couldn't see anywhere where she could kiss me. When Trevor drove her home, she was very quiet.

"Are you okay?" he asked her.

"Daddy didn't tell me how bad Mummy was," she said.

Trevor answered, "You would look like that if you had hit your head on the pavement, wouldn't you?"

She was silent for a minute before she said, "Yes." After that she perked up and was her usual chatty self.

Weeks of recovery

Dr Stan told Howard I would be in intensive care for a couple of weeks. But I was out and upstairs in a room by myself on Monday, only a couple of days after the attack. My room was overflowing with love from so many people. There were flowers, flowers and even more flowers. The staff had to provide an ambulance gurney as extra furniture to hold all the bouquets. Flowers just kept coming. In the end, having read who each bunch was from, I asked my family to take them home because there was no more space. I also gave them to people around the ward who had none. I was so blessed by these flowers and I thank all the people who showed me so much love. With so many bouquets in my room, the nurses were worried that they would not be able to get me out if there was an emergency!

Somehow, my beloved Howard survived the ten weeks I was in hospital. He would bring my clean washing to the hospital on his way to work at 6 a.m., having got the family up, and then do a full day's work. At night he would feed the family with a meal provided by our church, Forrest Hill Presbyterian, who kept us fed four nights every week for 16 weeks. My dear friend Judy arranged the roster. What amazing love! To this day, we are so grateful for the love and care they showed us. After dinner, Howard would bundle the family into the car, come and see me for about an hour, then take them home and put Allison to bed. He would clean up the dishes and drop into bed and do it all over again the next day. On his visits I could see how tired he was becoming. We arranged for a friend's daughter, Caroline, to come over and be with Allison when she got home from school. Our friend also did some cleaning and washing. She was a great help. Meanwhile, the amazing thing about all of this is that, throughout the entire stay in hospital, I had a peace that I can only describe as supernatural.

When I was put in a room by myself, my bed linen had to be replaced for the first time. It took eight nurses to lift me with the bottom sheet while another nurse put the clean sheet underneath and tucked it in. Then they laid me down and removed the old sheet. It was just like clockwork – everyone knew what they had to do. They had to call upon a nurse from another ward for support. When they went to lift me, this nurse said, "You can help by pulling up on the handrail above you." Only too happy to assist, I pulled as instructed, only to have excruciating pain shoot through my pelvis. With a cry of pain I let go of the handle and fell back onto the sheet that I was being lifted up with. The same nurse berated me for putting all my weight onto them which gave them bad backs. After that they all went back to what they had to do while my nurse made sure I was comfortable. From the look on the faces of the others, I have no doubt the outspoken nurse was told off.

The day arrived for my stitches to be removed. The ones on my forehead had been removed only a few days after the attack as they healed very quickly. Those to be taken out now were the stitches down my left leg – 35 staples which unfortunately were covered in dried blood. When the nurse started taking them out, the pain was horrendous. I was shaking from head to toe, eyes watering as this was accomplished. In hindsight it would have been a good idea to wash the dried blood away first. I am convinced this is what caused my agony.

A few weeks later I experienced pain in my groin. I spoke to Dr Stan about it because I thought the business of changing my sheets had upset the fractures in that part of my body. He said, "You don't have breaks there", but after checking the X-rays he confirmed that I did indeed have fractures. He prescribed the anti-inflammatory drug Voltaren which upset my stomach dreadfully. It was stopped the next day; after that there was no pain. Throughout my stay in hospital I was happy! I had publicly forgiven Richard, and my words about this had been published in the *New Zealand Herald*. Forgiveness set me free from harbouring anger and bitterness. I told Howard that I wanted to go and see Richard, and he agreed to take me when I was well enough.

There were many people who wrote to me with encouraging words. One I remember in particular was a gentleman in a holding cell at the Auckland police station. It was approximately the 30th time he had been charged for protesting outside the abortion clinic. He wrote about meeting Richard, my attacker: "The cell door opened and the policeman ushered in a young man who was very dark in spirit. I had been reading my Bible while I was waiting. The young man was Richard who asked me, 'Are you reading the Bible?' I said I was and spent the next half hour sharing Jesus with him. I offered to send him a Bible but he declined. The door opened and they took him out. That was the last I saw of Richard."

Another letter I received later on was from a young man called Reese. He wrote saying that when Richard was in the woodwork centre at Carrington Psychiatric Hospital, one of his supervisors was a Christian and had been able to speak to him, having heard through media reports that I had forgiven him. Reese told me that while Richard was on remand in Mount Eden Prison he was assaulted by two inmates for what he had done. He wrote: "Typical of Richard – he said he probably deserved the beating and did not feel anger towards the inmates. He just didn't know why he had done such a terrible act."

Reese said that over a period of six months he observed Richard slowly working through the crime he had committed, with the help of his Christian supervisor. The day before Richard died his supervisor was driving past Carrington, when he heard the quiet voice of God saying, "Go and see Richard." He thought it was a random idea and dismissed it, expecting to see Richard the following week. The next day, however, Richard withdrew all his money, left it on his bed and caught the bus from Point Chevalier to the City, where he jumped out of the 14th storey of the government building not far from where he had attacked me about three years previously.

A reporter rang to tell me Richard had taken his own life. I was saddened by this news as I thought it was such a waste of a young man's life. I sent the family a card and received a lovely card in return. I also met a psychologist who told me he had been seeing Richard and that Richard was very remorseful.

I never did get to meet Richard face to face after the attack. But I'm thankful he knew I had forgiven him.

CHAPTER TWO

Hospital Life

The first week I was in hospital my pastor, the Rev Alastair Smales, told me about a man called Tark who was in another room just down the hall from me. Tark, his wife, their children and his mother had been in a terrible car accident around the same time I had been attacked. They had recently become Christians and Alastair was visiting us both.

I started to communicate with Tark via the nurses. I wrote encouraging notes which the nurses then gave to him and he sent messages back. We communicated for a while without ever seeing each other. Then one day I was waiting for an X-ray, when I noticed a Māori man in a bed down the corridor. I asked him if he was Tark and he said "Yes." I told him I was Trixie and we started to talk. From then on, each time he was wheeled past my room he would call out a greeting to me. It was wonderful for me to be able to encourage him, and he me.

Tark's injuries weren't just physical. His mother had been seriously injured in the car accident and later died. They also lost both their children. His wife was injured and was in hospital too but was able to go home after a week or two. Whenever she visited Tark, she would come and see me. What a blessing she was. On the morning of her mother-in-law's funeral she came to say hello. I was feeling pretty down about the length of my hospital stay and unfortunately I didn't do much to encourage her – it was all about me, not her and the sad day she and her family were about to experience. How selfish of me. There are times, and this was one of them, when I regret my actions and words. This experience taught me that there is always someone worse off than me, and I am grateful for the lesson.

When I got out of hospital, I would sometimes see Tark at North Shore Hospital where we were both receiving physio treatment. It was always good to catch up. Tark and his wife had another baby even though the doctors had recommended against it. The couple believed God had said it would be okay, and it was. They named this little blessing 'Hope' and Allison and I went to her christening. Then the family shifted to Northland and we have lost contact.

Routines of hospital life

During my stay in Auckland Hospital, the nurses were exceptional with their care. I especially remember one called Pip. She arranged for me to have a shower, which was confusing to say the least as I couldn't stand up, but I was very excited just thinking about it. Until then I had only been having bed baths. This was the *crème de la crème* – a real luxury for me. Pip wheeled a shower bed into my room and then it took eight nurses to get me onto the contraption. She wheeled me away to the shower room and lowered the middle of the bed so that it sank down and as she showered me it became like a shallow bath. What bliss! I felt like a new woman.

Unfortunately, at that time the 'powers that be' were cutting down on staff numbers so that was the end of my showers... until I talked my beloved into doing it instead, which he did! With the help of a few willing visitors, Howard managed to get me lifted onto the shower bed so that he could wheel me away into the shower room. Allison thought this was so cool. She spent the time, unbeknown to us, giving the other five ladies in my room and their visitors a running commentary of what was taking place – "Now he is washing her hair," etc. She had everyone in stitches. There are some delightful experiences I will never forget about our children's visits.

Chris, our eldest, had a full-time job so couldn't visit me during the day. He liked it to be just him and me. One night he decided to come after lights out. He waited until security was out of sight, ran up the eight flights of stairs, and thought he had snuck in to my bedside without being seen. The next minute the night nurse was at the foot of the bed, looking very cross. She had spotted Chris with his shoulder-length hair and leather jacket with tassels down each arm and had followed him through the ward. After he politely explained that all he wanted was to talk to his mum, she relented and allowed us to have 20 minutes – but "NO LONGER!" That was a very special time for me.

Another time, Chris took me in my bed down to the hospital main entrance where there were people coming and going. I laughed as he turned the bed around and around. It was so nice to see the world instead of the inside of my room and once again I felt like a new woman.

Our other son Trevor had just got his driver's licence. He would come and order my meals for the next day then be there to feed me. He was always so gentle and sensitive to my needs. He has a great sense of humour and would always make me laugh. Allison came to visit on Saturday mornings. Howard would drop her off for two hours to spend time with me alone because I noticed she was not able to chatter to me as she would have liked each evening when her daddy and brothers were there. Saturday morning was our special time together. She would pump the bed up and down, up and down, while I laughed. The nurses sometimes dressed her up in surgical garb and she walked around talking to everyone, seeing visitors to the lift and saying, "Thank you for coming, please come again." In this special time we were able to have lovely long cuddles while she lay beside me.

My friend Judy was visiting one day when I was handed a hospital brown paper bag. They said it contained the clothes I had worn on the day of the attack. Judy, kind soul, asked if she could take them and dispose of them. I agreed without looking at them. Another day she was visiting our home when Trevor answered the door to a courier who gave him my watch which was covered in blood. Trevor found this pretty traumatic. Thank goodness Judy was there once again.

When I had been home for quite a while I answered the door to find someone holding another hospital bag and saying the clothes inside were mine. I took them, said thank you, and promptly put the bag down to answer the phone. It was my sister Lucy. While talking to her I started to feel very uncomfortable and felt I should go and find Allison, so I said my goodbyes. I found my darling little girl sitting in a chair holding my torn, bloodied clothes in her lap and very upset. Of course, a parcel being delivered was very interesting to an inquisitive little girl. It was my fault; I should have put the bag somewhere before answering the phone. My poor little girl, how could they get it so wrong? I have no idea who the other bag given to me in the hospital belonged to, but these clothes really were mine and they were not nice to look at.

Most of the nurses gave me excellent and, in some cases, outstanding care but I feel I need to mention a number of important exceptions. At one time there were a number of very elderly ladies in my room who were really unsettled. A couple of times I witnessed some dear ones who needed to use the bed pan. One woman waited for one and a half hours before she had a pan brought to her. By that time she was groaning to herself. Another lady got out of bed and wet the floor, only to be told off by a nurse. A 90-year-old woman who had a cracked pelvis and was very disorientated kept getting out of bed and hanging onto the edge of it as she made her way to the end. On one occasion when putting her back to bed, the nurse –

clearly frustrated – picked her up, held her over the bed and dropped her, not from a great height but enough to cause her dreadful pain.

I grew more and more upset at the mistreatment going on. One night I awoke to groaning from the bed next to me. The dear soul had asked for a bed pan, which they gave her, but that's where they left her. She was skin and bone; it was obviously very uncomfortable. I told her to ring again, and again. Finally two nurses walked in the door. As they came up to her bed one said, "Well, lift yourself up." They did what was necessary and one came down to the hand basin at the foot of my bed to wash her hands. She knew I was awake and had been observing what was going on. She gave me a look, then left.

The next morning while a trainee nurse was helping me get ready for the day, I asked her how to make a complaint. She got the charge nurse to come and see me and I related to her all that I had witnessed over the past week. She said, "Trixie, we have had people complain before but they won't put their name to the complaint and we are not able to do anything unless we have a name. Will you put your name to this complaint?" I assured her I would.

My poor husband had been saying to me, "You have another five weeks to go in here so you don't want to make enemies," but I had seen enough and I couldn't take any more. I knew I was in God's hands and that His protection was on me.

The charge nurse came and saw me again to say she had spoken to the nurses involved. One was from another ward and wouldn't be back. The other had recently had a smash in her car and her husband had been made redundant. This nurse had explained that she knew her behaviour was no excuse and that a nurse should leave all personal problems behind before she came to work. This is a big ask. I don't think I could do this, which is probably why I am not a nurse. The charge nurse also said that this particular nurse wouldn't be on duty for a couple of days.

At 3 p.m. that particular nurse walked past the ward door. She backtracked and gave me a big smile, then said very nicely, "Hello Trixie." I replied with an equally nice "Hello." When she had signed in she came to see me and brought me a couple of little cakes. She said she was sorry. That night as she was getting me ready for sleep, she made certain that I was comfortable, making sure that my leg was completely straight so that it wouldn't ache.

A few nights later I woke to find the night nurse standing at the foot of my bed just looking at me, so I looked back. It was dark – I have no idea if she could see I was awake. Anyway, she stood there for about five minutes while I prayed quietly to God for His protection. Although making a complaint may not have made me popular with the nurses involved, I wouldn't hesitate to speak up if the situation arose again. I am happy to say there were no repercussions from my lovely nurses; they were all very professional.

Dr Stan went on holiday for a week and left his interns in charge of me. The day after he left, the two interns arrived and said they were going to start me on a course of injections to stop my blood from clotting, which was a likely result of being immobile. They injected a blood thinner into my stomach a few times a day for the rest of the week. When Dr Stan came back he was not impressed with what they had ordered. He stopped the injections immediately and said I didn't need them, I would be fine – and I was! Thank you Dr Stan.

I could see my left leg getting very skinny and my right not far behind it, so I asked if a physiotherapist could come and give me exercises to strengthen my right leg so I wouldn't crumple into a big heap when it was time for me to start walking again. I had no idea it would take months until I could bear any weight on my left leg. A physio arrived soon after that and began visiting once a week. I got into the routine of doing exercises with my right leg, for which I am very grateful. Also in our church I had a friend, Helen, who was a physio and she used to come over and help me too. When I did become mobile I found my right leg had to take the weight of my whole body.

Back on my feet

The milestone of nine weeks arrived and they started to prepare me to become upright again. First I had to have the second rod which was protruding from each side of my leg taken out. I didn't like the thought of this happening so I asked for something to numb the leg, which they gave me. It sent me into space and I have no recollection of what happened. When I became aware of everything around me again I realised I was talking nineteen to the dozen. I asked a nurse what I had been saying and was told, "You wouldn't want to know." I do remember seeing a cork on the window sill before I went 'under'. That sight, plus the sedative, took me back to the days when I drank whisky on the rocks. That may have been funny for everyone there but it's something I like to forget.

After that, I had to get used to sitting up. A nurse commented that I would probably faint when I did sit up for the first time. I replied, "No I won't!" – and I didn't. They sat me in a La-Z-Boy chair next to the bed for short spells and gave me a rubber ring to sit on as my pelvic area was still very sore. From the chair I was able to see so much more. After I had mastered this they brought in a walking frame; it was huge and very sturdy. The first time I managed to hop from the end of my bed to the bed opposite and back. The feeling of achievement was amazing. Gradually I managed to go as far as the door and back.

Each time Howard came to visit in the evening I was bursting to tell him the good news. "I am coming home very soon – hooray!" To be able to stand up in a shower was remarkable and there was always a nurse to make sure I didn't faint in the process. They were so good to me. Dr Stan had said it would take more than a week to become strong enough to use crutches and then I could leave the hospital. I am pretty sure it only took a week and two days. After that, I was out of there!

A few days beforehand, the occupational therapist had been to my home to make sure everything was ready for my return. She took me for the ride and I sat in the car while she checked the house. Driving down the road felt like I was on the Pukekohe race track. I'm usually a speed freak but I had to ask her to slow down, which she did, apologising in the process. The day had finally arrived for me to go home.

CHAPTER THREE

Coming Home

The day I was to leave the hospital, Jane the occupational therapist taught me how to use crutches. As she wheeled me around to the three stairs opposite the lifts, she saw I was very anxious and asked if I was okay. When I said no, she decided to show me how to get to the top and down again. She asked if I would like to do it and, feeling determined, I climbed up the three stairs. I stood at the top with Jane hanging onto me, shaking and in total fear of the height. I then had a revelation as to what was happening: Satan was having a go at me, aiming to keep me in fear so that I would not be able to enjoy heights. Right there, I spoke out loud to him. "Get behind me, Satan. You have no authority over me. I am covered by the blood of Jesus. Go, in Jesus' name!" The tears stopped, the shaking stopped, and I had no more fear.

It was then I realised that the therapist was draped around my waist, crying. She said, "Oh Trixie, He really is real, isn't He?" We stood there hugging each other for a moment before I proceeded down the stairs, no problem.

Howard arrived, we said our goodbyes and a big thank you to the staff who had taken such good care of me, and off we went home. This is what I had been dreaming about for 10 weeks. They got me into the house with a fireman's lift and I was promptly put to bed exhausted. My goodness, I was tired – but very happy. What excited me even more was that I could be with my family all day, every day. I was able to get out of bed when I felt like it and sit in my own lounge – what joy!

ACC was helpful in arranging everything I needed to live at home. Howard took the first week off work to help me shower and he kept the house ticking over. He is such a gem of a man. I can't imagine going through this experience without him – such a rock and always thoughtful, always there when I needed him. The woman ACC had arranged to help came after a week and took over this job and also did the cleaning. The meals from Forrest Hill Presbyterian church continued for a further four weeks.

From this point, I progressed quite quickly. ACC was going to put a lift on the outside stairs so I would be able to get to the hospital for my physiotherapy exercises. Because I was getting stronger by the day I asked them to put a concrete path down the side of the house and a railing on the back steps instead, making it much easier for me to come and go and much cheaper than a lift. I was not driving at this stage so I had to rely on friends and family to get me to and from the hospital. The hospital offered to pick me up each day with their bus but the thought of going from house to house picking other people up and then having to drop them off on the way home was too much for me to consider. I was so tired after each visit I couldn't wait to get to bed.

My recovery was very quick. Howard took me to church each week in a wheelchair. Before long, I used crutches, then just one crutch, then nothing. My progress astounded the medical profession and all my family and friends. While I was in hospital a friend of my sister-in-law Joan saw a vision in which I fell from the bridge and returned to the top again. She told me, "God is going to restore you."

Around this time I had the rod down my left leg taken out. It had been painful and uncomfortable to lie on my side as there was not much body fat covering the rod and it pinched the skin. This time I went into the Southern Cross Hospital on Auckland's North Shore and the experience was very painful. The wound where the 35 staples had been had to be opened again, but fortunately this time there was no dried blood and there were stitches instead of staples.

It was good to have the rod out, but one leg was now shorter than the other and I waddled like a penguin. I was once again on crutches, which upset my back, and I was struggling.

During an Aglow meeting, three pastors gathered around and prayed for my healing. A friend had asked me to pray through her house to cleanse and bless it. So, after the meeting, I went to visit her. As I prayed from room to room, I realised I wasn't limping! When I left the house, I was able to walk down the front steps normally, without hanging on to the handrail with both hands. When I shared what had happened, my friends were overjoyed and rejoiced with me at the miracle.

A few days later, I went swimming with the family and they were excited to see their mother walking out of the water without assistance.

There is still a small difference in the length of my legs but it hasn't given me any difficulties since. As Jeremiah 17:14 says, "Heal me, Lord, and I will be healed; save me and I will be saved, for you are the one I praise."

Hepatitis C

In the first few years after the attack, I experienced debilitating tiredness. I would get the family off to work and school, then go back to bed. In the afternoon it was nothing for me to sleep for two to three hours and I was often in bed again at 8:30 p.m. I accepted this, realising my body had been through a lot and needed the sleep.

Christopher had his 21st birthday party at home and I did the catering. This was a mammoth task when I was so tired every day but I did it. Two years later it was Trevor's turn. During Chris's party I went out on the front deck to find Howard, who was talking to our friends. I stood beside him waiting to ask him a question when all of a sudden everything went black and I sank to the deck. Howard grabbed me, took me inside and sat me down. I felt terrible and was very white. He then put me to bed. I had never fainted before in my life so this caused us considerable concern.

The following Monday I went to see my doctor who asked if I had had blood transfusions while in hospital. I said, "Yes." He sent me to a specialist who researched the hospital archives. He called Howard and me back to his surgery and told us I had received bad blood. As a result, I now had hepatitis C. The specialist told us that people react to the disease in different ways: some die within three months of receiving infected blood; some experience tiredness; and others notice no symptoms at all. We decided I definitely had the tiredness. The specialist was wonderful, very forward-thinking. He wrote a letter, putting it on record that I had received bad blood from transfusions and would be a candidate for any future cure for this disease.

It took until 2016 for his words to come to pass. I have spent the last 27 years believing I am healed of this horrible disease. God says in the Bible that by His stripes we *are* healed, not we will be healed, and I believe what the Bible says. I was prayed for by a woman from New York about ten years later and from then on I had spoken out my healing – "I am healed."

Following the diagnosis, however, I grew progressively slower until I was not able to do very much at all because of chronic tiredness. I was still having liver function blood tests every six months and in the back of my mind was the awareness that if I was healed, the doctor would have told me so. But I am a person who does not give in easily – I still proclaimed my healing.

Later on I had some trouble with my heart. I was put on heart tablets but they did me no good and in fact I nearly died three times while on them. I went back to the specialist, who took me off them. We sought a second opinion and both specialists said I should not have been on those tablets in the first place as people had been dying while taking them. I transferred from private care to the public health system. The cardiologist I saw at the hospital said, "I don't think it is your heart which is the problem, I think it is the hep C." Wow! Both Howard and I were taken aback – we hadn't thought of this. After consulting with my GP, we met with an endocrinologist. He advised us that there were new trials being done for hep C and it wouldn't be long before this disease would be eliminated from society.

Shortly after this, our son Trevor happened to watch a television programme about hepatitis. He rang us, saying he and his wife would write to the professor who had been on the programme and we should write to my doctor about it. Trevor's wife Wendy is a cardiac nurse – an added bonus when it comes to medical matters! So we wrote, filling him in about the attack and why I had had to have transfusions. The professor and my doctor got in touch and, together, made my case with ACC. Before long, ACC rang me to say I was covered. The family was overjoyed. They had been watching their wife, mum and nana getting old before their eyes. Nana on the other hand was not so sure.

I firmly believe that God can and does heal supernaturally and that He also uses the medical profession. I had claimed God's healing for many years in recovering from the attack but also through various other medical crises, including breast and bowel cancer and blood clots in both lungs. I had faced death six times but now I had reached the stage where I had had enough. I had been cut open, sewed up, prodded and poked so many times I just wanted to be left alone. I didn't want to go through anything else. I talked myself into the thought that God did not want me to have treatment for hepatitis, which was nonsense. My beloved was very gentle with me and said he thought I should go and speak to a pastor. What would I do without Howard?

I made an appointment with Pastor Kim at City Impact North Shore, the church we joined when we returned to Auckland after living in Nelson. She is a very wise and insightful woman. I took Allison along with me and I explained what I was feeling. She never said I was wrong, just very gently suggested that God does work through the medical profession. I knew this and had no argument with it. Secondly, she said Howard and I should be in unity over this decision (we were not). Thirdly, she asked what I thought God was saying about it. I had not asked Him; I had just gone off on my own tangent. All these things I knew but I was so tired of people in the medical world, I just wanted it all to stop. I went home to seek guidance, which I received very quickly and clearly. Yes I was to go ahead with the treatment and He would be with me all the way. "Thank you Jesus!"

The lesson in all of this is no matter how mature I think I am spiritually, I can still go off on a tangent when I do not seek the Lord's will for my life. Why am I baring my soul? I hope it will help and encourage others that our God knows the best for us in all circumstances.

The treatment was to take three months – a tablet once a day, every day. The side effects were minimal with this particular drug, called Harvoni. The first day I experienced huge resistance when I held the tablet in my hand. I said to Howard, "I don't want to do this, but I will." It got easier each day. I started to get headaches so I drank water. From then on I just drank and drank. At the end of the three months I was drinking five and a half litres a day. Yes, I was going to the bathroom a lot but it was worth it!

As time progressed we noticed I was able to go up our stairs at home with no effort. Before this I hated our three-storeyed house because having to pull myself up the stairs was such an effort. Even taking our bedspread off the bed and putting it on again took all my energy. Now, though, I even enjoyed hanging out the washing. I had been taking the easy option and putting it in the dryer. Little changes were becoming obvious and it was very exciting.

In October 2016 I celebrated my 70th birthday and our 50th wedding anniversary. For my birthday the family arranged for me to fly in a helicopter from Albany to Auckland, around the Sky Tower, Devonport, Rangitoto, and out to Waiheke Island where all the family were waiting to share a scrumptious lunch with Howard and me at Cable Bay. We all came back on the ferry at the end of a very long day. What was so amazing was that I was able to do this without getting tired!

On 8 December 2016 I received confirmation from the hospital of what I had believed for nearly 30 years. Having completed the Harvoni treatment programme, I was now healed of hepatitis C. Thank you Lord!

PART TWO

The Episodes of Life

CHAPTER ONE

Beginnings

I grew up in the picturesque suburb of Northcote Point, on Auckland's North Shore. There were seven of us – six girls and one boy, and I am the youngest. Now there are five girls, as my dear sister Meriel took her life when she was 42 and I was 39 years old.

We grew up with a father who had an anger problem. My older siblings were on the receiving end of this more than I was. They tell me I was the 'spoilt one'. There are 15 years between me and my oldest sister Airdre.

When I was three years old, I used to go for walks with my paternal grandfather. I rode my little tricycle and he walked beside me. One day, my mother and I were boarding a bus when the driver said, "Good to see Trixie again – and looking so healthy and well."

My mother looked puzzled and asked him what he was referring to.

"Did your father-in-law not tell you what happened the other day?" he said.

"No!" Mum replied very firmly. "Tell me about it."

The driver went on to explain that he had been driving the bus, loaded with passengers, up the hill from the ferry when he saw me hurtling down the footpath the other way. He stopped the bus, jumped out and managed to grab me just as I was about to go over the curb at full speed, saving me from a very nasty tumble amongst cars and buses.

Poor Mum had no idea this had happened. When she got home and tackled Granddad about it, he said, "Oh, there was no need to worry. I knew someone would stop her. I had just stopped to tie up my shoelace when she took off. I knew I couldn't stop her." I think Mum forbade him from taking me anywhere near that hill again. I have no recollection of the event myself but I suspect I was having fun as I have always loved speed and heights.

Northcote was a wonderful place for children. We had five beaches to choose from. If the wind was coming in on one side of the point, we swam on the other. The Auckland Harbour Bridge was built while I was in primary school. Unfortunately, that took away some of our beaches but it didn't stop us having fun. The older children had tied a rope swing to the handrail of the approach to the bridge. After climbing up a cliff, and out onto the limb of a pōhutukawa tree, we would swing out under the approach and then drop off into the water.

Not all my memories from those days are sunny. I was molested as a little girl – not often, but it did happen – and there was also groping. There are probably other women reading this who have suffered much worse. My experiences were more than enough to mess up my life until God healed me. I know He is able to do the same for you, as you get to know Him. He created you, knows you intimately and can heal you of any past hurts.

Despite these difficulties, I was a happy child, always singing and whistling as I went about the Point. I would talk to everyone wherever I went. My mother would come across people who would say things like, "Oh, so you're Trixie's mother. We met her the other day when she knocked on our door wanting to use our toilet on the way home from school." I was very curious to see what people's houses looked like inside.

When Billy Graham came to New Zealand on one of his evangelistic crusades in the early 1960s, I went to his meeting with my parents. I was 15 years old. I wanted to become a Christian but because no one asked me, I thought I had missed the opportunity and I was quite sad. Our family attended Northcote Methodist Church and during the service the following Sunday, the pastor asked anyone who would like to accept Jesus into their life to come forward. I couldn't wait to get up the front – I was so excited that I hadn't missed out! Unfortunately my teenage years were all about going with the flow and I am sad to say it was not a very nice flow.

CHAPTER TWO

Married to a Wonderful Man

While still in my teens, I tried many different jobs. I think I had 11 before I was married. I did a shorthand typing course purely so I could leave school. I was going to be a secretary, dress in nice clothes and earn lots of money. Unfortunately, while I could take dictation well enough, transcribing it on the typewriter was a problem because my spelling ability was terrible (and still is). The spelling of some words was such a mystery to me that I couldn't even find them in the dictionary and, unfortunately, we didn't have computers to correct our mistakes in those days. I loved to type but only if I was copying something. There was no problem with that. However, my future as a secretary was short-lived.

After I got married the job I enjoyed most was driving a dry-cleaning van around the North Shore. When I was out on the road I felt like the day was my own. I made friends with most of the clients as I picked up and dropped off their items. I was good behind the wheel and drove a Morris van. I had no problem backing up long driveways – except when they were gravel and very steep – because the van was quite light in the back. One day, after I had delivered dry-cleaning to one woman, I had to ask her to sit in the back of the van to add weight so I could get up the very steep road. She very kindly did so. I don't think I went back to pick up clothes from her again – I wonder why?

I was asked by my boss's wife to pick strawberries for her while out doing my deliveries. I pulled into the car park and left my van with doors unlocked and my money bag on the front seat. I trusted everyone. Needless to say, the bag wasn't there when I got back. My boss was not happy with me, or with his wife for asking me to pick strawberries when I should have been working. I never stopped to consider that I should not be doing this. If someone in authority asked me to do something for them, I did it and never questioned it. All through my life I have obeyed and done what I have been asked, even to my own detriment.

In 1966 at the age of 20, I married the most loving and understanding husband anyone could wish for. Howard and I had met while working for TEAL (as Air New Zealand was known in those days). I had often seen him in the cargo department, this handsome dude in his smart uniform, but I had no idea who he was. I was one of the telephonists; apparently he had seen me strutting along the street in my stilettos. One day, he rang after 5 p.m. to make a toll call. I asked him his surname.

"Jellie," he said.

It sounded more like a dessert than a surname. "You're joking," I replied. There was silence on the other end of the line. I quickly recovered my professional demeanour. "Oh I am so sorry, I will put you through."

Shortly afterwards the door opened and in he came, wanting to meet the cheeky telephonist. The rest is history...

We have three children – two boys born two years apart, Christopher and Trevor, and then our extra blessing, a girl named Allison, born eight years later. All our children celebrate their birthdays during the same week in November. They all married within a year – one in February 2001 and the other two the following February. We now have six beautiful grandchildren we are so proud of, and they were all born within a period of four years.

I started going to church when our eldest was six years old but my Christianity was just on the surface. Mostly I did my own thing and didn't give much thought to God. Four years later I realised that I was empty inside and only Jesus could fill the gap. I went to my pastor at Forrest Hill Presbyterian Church and told him how I was feeling. He helped me see the emptiness within me and then I prayed a prayer asking Jesus to forgive me for leaving Him out of my life and to fill me with His love, which He did. From that day on, my life was transformed. I knew for certain that I was God's child and I felt bathed in His love.

My rediscovered faith was confirmed by the following experience. Allison had started walking at the age of nine months. By the time she was eleven months old she was walking everywhere and was extremely active. One day when I was talking to someone on the phone, I heard the Lord's audible voice saying to me, "Allison has the Janola bottle." It was as if Jesus was standing next to me. Everything had gone quiet and I felt His presence surrounding me. Janola is a strong household bleach that could severely injure a child if they drank it. I dropped the phone and ran through the house to the laundry where I found my little girl with the Janola bottle between her legs and the lid off, smiling, always smiling. From that day on I have never doubted that my God is real and that no matter what I go through, He will always be there for me.

In 1983 when Allison was three years old, we shifted to the house next door. Our neighbour's marriage had folded; we had two boys with a lot of energy and this house had a huge bedroom for them as well as a large pool and spa. Our neighbour had come over for dinner and during the course of the meal suggested, "You should buy my house." After talking about it for the next few days, we asked him if we could have a look through. We had been in the house often although not as prospective buyers. He was going away for the weekend so left the keys with us. Howard thought there was so much work needing to be done and we had just been through the process of renovating our existing home. I, on the other hand, could see all the extra room we needed for our growing family. Howard began looking at other houses that required less maintenance while I took the matter to God in prayer.

Later that weekend when we finally took the family to see the neighbour's house, the boys were ecstatic. We came home and talked about it. I said I thought we should pray and Howard agreed. I said a prayer, something like this: "Thank you Lord for this opportunity. Lord, we are undecided what to do. Father, I am placing a fleece before you, as Gideon did (Judges 6:36-40). Our neighbour has the house on the market for $95,000, but we can only afford $85,000. If we are to shift, I pray that our neighbour will accept $85,000 without any hesitation."

Howard went next door on Monday night to return the keys. The neighbour didn't invite him in as he usually did but stepped out onto the front steps. Howard said, "We looked at the house and thought we could live here." Without any prompting, the man replied that he wouldn't accept anything less than $85,000. Wow! Howard nearly fell off the steps. I said, "Thank you, Lord!" and we made a firm offer. It was a great home for the children to grow up in and they all have fond memories of living there.

CHAPTER THREE

A Growing Faith

Three days before my 39th birthday my sister Meriel died. She was 42 and had taken her own life. I was still a young Christian at this time and often think, "If only I had known then what I know now." However, I believe that God is God and He holds everything in His hands. He knows the pain and suffering our family went through as a result of this tragic loss and as I look back now, I can see I grew through my time of grief. God never wastes anything. We may come across someone in a similar situation someday whom we may be able to help, and this was so for me.

A year later, I was at an Aglow meeting with my mum. Aglow is a Christian organisation for people of all church denominations. It was the anniversary of Meriel's death and Mum asked for prayer as she was grieving terribly that day. I walked past as she was being ministered to and the Lord gave me a word for her so I went over and spoke the message out: "I gave her to you, you brought her up, but now it's time to give her back to me." Later, she said it was those words that enabled her to trust God and let Meriel go.

A parent who loves the Lord always wants their child to become a child of God. It is the greatest blessing to know that you will be reunited with your children some day in heaven. I feel the same way about all my family members. I believe that I will see Meriel again. Ultimately, only God knows what a person may have called out in their last moments but I know He is merciful and loves everyone who calls on Him, unconditionally. "Everyone who calls on the name of the Lord will be saved" (Romans 10:13).

When I was helping sort through Meriel's things, I found she had cut out this verse from Matthew 6:25-26 and put it in her wallet: "Therefore I tell you, do not worry about your life, what you will eat or drink; or about your body, what you will wear. Is not life more than food and the body more than clothes?" I have hope that she cried out to God and He heard her.

Protected by God

I had to go into a private hospital in Takapuna for a prolapsed uterus. The day before I was admitted, my mum came around to visit. When she sat on the couch in the lounge, the leg of the couch went through the carpet and through the floor. Poor dear, it gave her quite a fright but I managed to turn it into something funny and we laughed and laughed. Howard came home and pulled back the carpet – the floor was very wet and soggy, just like Weetbix! The wooden framed windows in the lounge had been leaking. It would be another big job for him to fix it. Mind you, he does like to have a project and that house certainly had many. The next day I had my operation and was in hospital for two days. When I came home, I found the carpet was rolled back about two metres and the floorboards had been removed so that you could see straight down into the workshop below.

That night I couldn't sleep so I got up and went out to the lounge. I always like the curtains open as the night sky fascinates me and I don't have to put the light on. The curtains had been left shut and, without thinking of the hole in the floor, I walked over and opened them. Then I went into the kitchen to have a drink before going back to bed.

In the morning, after Howard had left for work, I came into the lounge and stared at the gaping hole in the floor. The realisation hit me: What on earth had I done last night and how had I not fallen into the cavernous workshop below? All I could do was praise my God for protecting me. I told my son Trevor what had happened and he was stunned. That night at the dinner table he asked if I had told Dad what I had done during the night. Poor Howard went white when I told him the story. He fixed the floor very quickly after that!

God's revelation

God is always interested in everything that is going on in our lives – even the little things. One Monday morning Howard couldn't find his car keys and became very anxious. He had looked everywhere and asked me to help. I went upstairs to the bedroom and asked the Holy Spirit where the keys were. I immediately had a mental picture of a suede coat that I had not seen Howard wear for a couple of years. I looked in the pocket and there they were.

Howard was very relieved when I handed him the keys. He asked me where I had found them. I told him and mentioned I hadn't seen him wearing that coat for a few years. "I tried the coat on during the weekend to see if it would still fit," he said. "How did you know the keys were there?" I told him God had given me a picture of the coat so I went and had a look.

Sharing Jesus with others

About three years after Meriel's death, I started up a business of my own as a window cleaner since Allison was now at school. I secured a job at one of the little houses in an old-style retirement village owned by the city council. An elderly gentleman there was in bed for the day. As I was cleaning his windows he made the comment: "I don't know where you get your energy from!"

"Oh, I get it from Jesus!" I said.

"Oh, you're one of those, are you?" he replied.

"I sure am. I wouldn't be here if it wasn't for Him." I told him a little of my story, which fascinated him. I was asked back the next day to clean the kitchen. At morning tea time he told me a bit about himself and how he had gone to church as a young man before he went off to war. At one time during the war, he had called out to God and received His peace. But when he came home he couldn't settle in a church and drifted away.

While I was listening, I heard God's still small voice say, "Invite him to Aglow tomorrow." I obeyed and when I made the invitation, the gentleman said "Yes" without any hesitation. When I was at home that night I started to doubt whether I had heard correctly because Aglow was a women's ministry at that time. I tried ringing the Aglow president to see what she thought but the line was engaged so I went back to peeling potatoes. I then heard God's voice saying, "Trust me" – so I did.

Next day when I went to collect the gentleman from his home, he was waiting at the side of the road, dressed in a reefer jacket and wearing his medals. I managed to get him up the stairs into the building where the meeting was held and asked him where he would like to sit. "Right down the front, please!" he replied.

The speaker was Pastor Mal Maloney from Belmont Baptist Church. The gentleman sat the whole time with his head in his hands and I thought he had gone to sleep. When he had finished speaking, Mal said, "This was not what I was going to speak on today but God told me to preach this message instead." Then, looking directly at the gentleman, he said, "And it was just for you, wasn't it?" The elderly man nodded. Mal asked him if he would like to come to the front and publicly acknowledge Jesus as his Lord and Saviour. Without hesitation the man jumped out of his seat and went straight up to Mal. As Mal prayed, there were probably about 150 women praying along with him.

Unfortunately, this man's wife didn't want to know about Jesus.

But he had made his peace with God and it wasn't long after this that he passed away. I am looking forward to meeting him again when I get to heaven. God's Word says, "But when He, the Spirit of truth, comes He will guide you into all the truth" (John 16:13). He certainly did for this lovely man. The lesson I learnt from this is that we must obey whenever God speaks – five minutes later may be too late.

CHAPTER FOUR

God at Work in a Rest Home

I eventually obtained a job as a nurse aide at a rest home in Birkenhead, job-sharing with my lovely friend Sandy. I love older people and they love me, and I would often pray for them when they asked me to.

I had been there for some time when I began to experience pain in my right knee, especially when I was walking up and down the stairs. I put up with this for some time, then suddenly the thought came to mind, "This is not from God, it is an attack," so I started claiming my healing. I put my hand on the knee and spoke out loud: "Satan, you have no authority in my body. I am healed by the blood of Jesus. Pain, you have to go, in the name of Jesus. Thank you Jesus for my healing." The pain didn't go straightaway but I continued to speak out this declaration whenever I felt it. After about three weeks the discomfort disappeared. I praised God and thanked Him so much. Some time later, the pain returned with force. I hobbled around for a day or so until I suddenly remembered and spoke out the declaration. This happened a few times until persistence won out and I have never had the problem since. Praise the Lord.

Paul

At the rest home there was a gentleman named Paul who was suffering from emphysema, having smoked for a good many years. I came on duty one day only to find he had been shifted to North

Shore Hospital. He had no one, except for a daughter in Australia – who never came to see him – and no friends visited, so I decided to call on him.

When I turned up in Paul's hospital room he was very pleased to see me and I visited whenever I could during the few weeks he was there. The nurses got used to me coming to visit and asked who I was. One day I asked Paul if he would like to invite Jesus into his life, as I had been sharing how I loved Jesus, and he said he would. I prayed with him and told him he was now my brother in Christ. I also said that if it was possible, I would be with him when his time came to be with Jesus. I called in one day to find him in a coma and I sat with him for about an hour. After a while the hospital chaplain came. We sat there talking about Jesus and how I came to know Paul and I told him Paul was now a follower of Jesus, so I would get to see him again. Eventually I had to leave to shop for groceries. I told Paul I would be back as soon as I could but when I returned to his room, I found the mattress rolled up and no Paul. A nurse saw me standing in the doorway and came to say that they were so sorry – they had been keeping an eye out for me but missed seeing me arrive. They hadn't intended for me to see Paul's room empty like that. She said he had passed away peacefully. Praise the Lord!

I was invited to a memorial service for Paul at the hospital. Three or four nurses attended. One spoke about what a lovely man he had been to nurse. I shared how I had spent time with him and had invited him to become a Christian, and said that I would like to sing a song that my sister had received from God during a storm while travelling on her yacht from Auckland to the Pacific Islands. First she received the tune – one which she didn't know her grandfather had often played on the organ. Then she was given the words. When I had finished singing the song, there were a few moist eyes among the nurses. It is great to know God will keep His promises and I know Paul and I will meet again.

Harry

While I was off duty one day, an elderly resident named Harry died. A few days after the funeral the owner of the rest home asked if I would take a small memorial service for the residents who had not been able to go to the funeral. Without thinking, I said, "Of course." When I realised the enormity of this decision I rang my pastor, Alastair Smales, and told him what I had been asked to do. He reassured me that I could do it and we talked about which Scriptures I could read. I looked in a hymn book that was used at the rest home and chose a couple of songs. My goodness – my knees were shaking but God got me through it. Everyone who attended said it was wonderful and I had done so well. Wow!

Stan

Another of the residents, named Stan, mentioned that he wasn't able to read and asked if I would come and read the Bible to him. After my shift had finished I would go in for half an hour and read to him. My friend Sandy had been having a bit of trouble with this man's dirty language while she showered him but I never had any trouble with him. I kept reading and prayed that the words would touch his heart. Even though I didn't see him make his peace with God, I am reminded to never underestimate the power of Scripture and the eternal impact it can have on someone's life.

After I left that job I would sometimes return there with a group of women from Aglow and we would share testimonies and have a sing-song of all the old hymns. The residents always really looked forward to this.

CHAPTER FIVE

Divine Interventions

I had been experiencing headaches for three weeks so I asked the prayer chain at church to pray for me. I couldn't work out why I was suffering in this way. One Sunday morning, I was getting my porridge ready before I set out for church. I was just about to add my sugar substitute when I heard a voice saying, "Don't have any more of that."

I thought to myself, "Was that God? Maybe not." I carried on and put the sugar substitute in.

I then heard these words: "I said don't have any more of that."

"Oh my goodness, Lord, I am so sorry, please forgive me." I tipped out the porridge and started again. By 3 p.m. I had no more headaches. For a long time after that, I couldn't have anything that was a diet product or anything with a sugar substitute in it because I would instantly get a migraine. It never ceases to amaze me how God is interested in the details and not only cares about our salvation but also our health and our daily lives.

Julie

About four weeks into my hospital stay after the attack, a lovely woman called Julie arrived. She had been hit by a car while riding her bicycle to work. Julie was in hospital for about five weeks and we grew very close while she was there. She had had a few very rough years and had tried all sorts of alternative things, trying to find peace. I talked to her about Jesus and gave her some leaflets to read. When she was being taken to theatre she asked me to pray for her. I replied, "Of course I will."

One night when we were talking, I said I was very tired and would see her in the morning. The next day she excitedly told me that while she had been waiting for sleep with her eyes shut, she had seen a very bright light. She asked me what I thought it could have been.

"Jesus is the light of the world," I said. "He was letting you know He really is real."

That night when the lights were out I said, "Julie, you don't need me to introduce you to Jesus. Just ask Him to come into your heart."

The next morning I looked at her and it was as if I was looking at a totally different person. She had peace written all over her.

"Trixie, guess what?" she said.

"You don't have to tell me," I said. "I can see it in your face. You have asked Jesus into your life."

It wasn't only me who noticed. My sister-in-law Joan came and asked me where the lady was who had been in the bed next to me. I pointed at Julie. Joan shook her head and said to me, "No, the lady who used to be there."

I said, "That's her."

Then the penny dropped. Joan turned to Julie and said, "You've met the Lord Jesus, haven't you?" We all rejoiced together. I see Julie every now and again and it is so good to see her growing in her faith.

God's heavenly language

The first Christmas after I was attacked, we rented a bach at Tairua on the Coromandel coast. Unfortunately, Chris had to work but Allison, Trevor and his friend – both aged 17 – came with us for two weeks' holiday. The weather was great and we had a wonderful time. The bach had a very steep drive which was difficult for me to get up without Howard's help but then I discovered that if I held onto our black labrador's tail, she would pull me up!

One day we went up the coast to Hot Water Beach. While we sat in a nice hot pool that Trevor and his mate had dug for us to soak in, they went into the surf for a swim. Not long afterwards, Howard jumped up and said the boys were in trouble. Looking out, we could see four waves rolling in, then a hand raised for help. Howard ran down the beach to a child (poor dear), took her flutter-board and went into the water. A tourist from the United Kingdom said he would go and help. As I stood there watching the two men swim out to the boys, a woman came up to me and said, "I'm a surf lifesaver, and there is no way I would go into that water. But I'll go to the shop and see if they have any rope."

While I watched the drama unfold, all I could pray was, "Oh God! Oh God!" Then the Holy Spirit took over and suddenly I was praying in another language. I didn't have to stop for breath; I was praying with power and authority. The experience of God's blessing was so strong and I knew He was answering my prayer.

Meanwhile, I kept watching as Howard and the tourist reached Trevor and his friend. Together the two men helped to bring the boys back to the beach. Trevor was tired but okay; his friend was totally washed out – no energy at all. We left them for a while to recover in the hot pool while we drove around to try and find the man who had helped so we could thank him properly. He had returned to the campground with his wife but we couldn't find them, and I still regret not being able to say a big thank you.

That night Trevor came into my bedroom to talk about the day. He said he knew I had been praying for them when they were in the water. He was okay but his friend had struggled as he was not a strong swimmer. Every time Trevor got close to him, his friend had dragged him down so Trevor swam alongside him, encouraging him. Then all of a sudden, Trevor said, he was lifted up by a wave and dumped on solid sand. He turned and grabbed his friend at the same time as his dad and the tourist arrived. God saved those boys that day and my prayer life went to a whole new level.

I had been prayed for at Aglow to be able to speak in tongues (God's heavenly language). I so loved God and desired everything He had for me but I didn't receive the gift immediately. I used to put on my ear phones and listen to music as I vacuumed the house. As I did this, I would often pray and ask God to help me pray in tongues and then I tried it out. With the earphones on and the vacuum cleaner going, I couldn't hear myself. It was probably not the way I should have approached it. My mind should have been centred on God and what I was praying for, not randomly opening my mouth and expecting God to fill it with divine inspiration but it was an exercise in trust.

In Jesus' name

At the beginning of the next year, I was asked to go to Rangitoto Island to share my story with the leaders of Auckland's Girls' Brigade who were having a retreat in a little bach there. When I look back, I realise I really had no idea what I was supposed to do. Anyway, I did my best. What I do remember is going to the out-side toilet in the dark of night, just before I was due to speak. As I came out of the toilet a tangible fear overcame me. It was the same fear that I had experienced when leaving hospital the year before. I moved as quickly as I could to the back door of the bach with this fear clinging to me. I had my hand on the latch, ready to burst in on these dear ladies, when I realised what was happening. So again I took the authority I have been given by Jesus and told the fear to go! Praise God, He is always faithful to those who trust in Him.

Encountering evil

After I was able to drive again, my dear friend Gwenda admitted herself into the Alcoholics Anonymous programme. This was held in the city, over the other side of the harbour bridge. Howard was a bit concerned about me driving to the city at night but I assured him I was being looked after, at which he smiled and said, "Be careful."

On Tuesday nights the AA group had chapel and on Friday nights they held their meeting – a time to share with others how they had managed to get through the week and overcome their problems. This was the first time I had been to an AA meeting. While everyone else went to get a cup of Milo for supper after the meeting, I sat alone in the middle of a row of seats. As I sat there I prayed, "Lord, you have brought me to support Gwenda; there must be someone else you want me to encourage. I am here alone in the middle of the room so you will have to bring them to me."

At that exact moment a Māori man with lots of bushy hair and tattoos turned and eye-balled me. "Thank you Lord!" I said silently as the man came towards me. He walked down the aisle then along the row in front of where I was sitting. Putting out his hand to shake mine, he said, "Hi, my name is Pete. I'm a Satanist."

I said, "Hi Pete, my name is Trixie and I love the Lord Jesus Christ. In fact I am a walking miracle of His grace. Someone attempted to murder me. I was attacked and thrown off the Mayoral Drive over-bridge one morning. You know what, Pete? I forgave him."

"Forgave him!" Pete said. "I would have ****** killed him."

So I said, "Pete, that's the difference between your god and mine. Mine is a God of love."

He gave me a long, hard look, nodded, and walked back to his friends. I never saw him again but every now and then the Lord brings him to mind. I pray for him, asking God's blessings upon him and praying that he will come to know the one true God of unconditional love.

Remembering Monique

On another occasion, during a Friday night meeting, a woman shared with everyone about how she had managed during the week. As she was speaking, I had a strong sense that I knew her. I asked the Holy Spirit, who reminded me where I had seen her before. He even gave me her name.

Her name was Monique and I had met her in hospital. She had suffered a compound fracture and I would often see her getting into a wheelchair so she could go outside and have a smoke. Her bed was opposite mine and I tried to reach out to her and talk to her about Jesus. She was not having a bar of it. She signed herself out very soon after her operation – I hope it wasn't because of me.

Now here she was at the AA meeting. She seemed so different from the woman I had seen in hospital and I wanted to speak to her. Afterwards, I couldn't find her so Gwenda went down to the bedroom block and brought her back to the hall. As they walked along the path below the deck I was standing on, I looked over the side and said, "Hi Monique, I don't suppose you remember me. I'm Trixie. I was in hospital with you." Monique gave an excited cry and ran up the stairs, picked me up and swung me around in a big bear hug. When she had quietened down she said, "I haven't been able to get you out of my mind since seeing you in hospital. All you did was love me. After all that had happened to you, you were reaching out to me in love. I just couldn't handle it."

I said, "What's the difference between the Monique I saw in hospital and the one I see now? You've changed."

She said, "Last night I knelt beside the bath and asked Jesus into my heart." Thank you Jesus!

We sow the seeds but it's God who waters them and makes them grow. After I reconnected with Monique, the church I attended, Forrest Hill Presbyterian, gave her many of the things she needed to set up house in Auckland. She was so blessed. Unfortunately, we have lost contact. I can only pray that she is growing in her love for Jesus.

A rainbow

Howard and I were coming home from our bach up north a few years ago when I had an incredible experience. We got to the Silverdale roundabout and as we came out on the other side of the overhead bridge, I noticed a small rainbow in the paddock to our right. I had never seen one so small – probably about the height of a two-storeyed house. Then, to my amazement, the rainbow moved directly in front of our car.

When we came to the first bridge over the motorway I thought to myself, "This is going to be interesting." But when we emerged out the other side, there it was again. It stayed with us for 19 kilometres, all the way to our exit by the Takapuna Golf Course. As we went up the ramp it suddenly disappeared. It took me quite a few years before I asked Howard if he had seen it – I wish I had asked him at the time – but then again, if he had seen it, he would surely have made a comment. It could only have been a 'God thing'. I was so excited and praised God in my heart when I saw it. To this day, I believe He gave me that rainbow to show me how much He loves me and is always with me. The rainbow is a sign of God's solemn promise to all living creatures, including humans, that He will never destroy all life with a flood again (Genesis 9:15-17).

CHAPTER SIX

Praying for Our Children

When Allison was seven years old, I found her crying in bed after I had tucked her in. She said she cried every night but didn't know why. I prayed for her but she still cried each evening. I discussed this with Howard and we decided I should take her for Christian counselling. I knew of a retired pastor who was a counsellor so Allison and I went to see him. He said he couldn't say for sure what it was that was causing Allison's tears but he felt it was something to do with her father. A little alarmed, I replied that her dad was a loving, caring daddy and that he worked long hours. I prayed about this for the rest of the week. On Sunday I sat down in church before the service and said to the Lord, "I have no idea what is causing this weeping in Allison but you do. Please would you reveal it to me?"

Instantly I had my answer, as a memory quickly came into my mind. When Allison was about three years old, Howard had made the comment to me about how beautiful she was, to which I replied, "You must never touch her in an inappropriate way." I was speaking out of the hurt within me from my own childhood experiences which, at that stage, I had not dealt with.

After the Holy Spirit revealed this to me, I asked Him to prepare Howard's heart and help me to speak to him about it. That night Howard and I were soaking in the spa and I said to him, "Do you find it hard to love and cuddle Allison?" He said he did but he didn't understand why. I then asked for his forgiveness for the words I had spoken over him about not touching her inappropriately. We talked about this for some time and he asked me how he could love her the way he was supposed to. I said, "By putting her on your knee and cuddling her and telling her how much you love her, how special she is to you."

What a transformation followed! Our little girl became so happy and couldn't wait for her daddy to come home each night for cuddles. Soon after, I remember seeing Howard and Allison lying on the floor watching the news side by side. This was how Howard liked to relax on a Friday night after a very hard week and it was wonderful to see the two of them together like that.

How true it is that our words can speak life or death. I didn't know this then but what a lesson I learnt through that experience. I pray that you too will be helped by our example. "Death and life are in the power of the tongue and those who indulge it will eat its fruit" (Proverbs 18:21, Amplified Bible). I will add that Howard and Allison now have such a close, loving relationship; in fact, years later, Allison told me she was looking for a husband just like her father. She did find a lovely man, Karl, who has godly wisdom. He is a wonderful husband and father and a wonderful son who has joined our family.

God-imparted knowledge

There were other occasions when the Lord would alert me to things that were going on in our children's lives so I could pray about them. Sometimes He would have me talk to the children about something He had shown me. The look on their faces each time was something to behold.

At such times I have felt the need to "stand in the gap" and intercede for my family, just as the Israelites had to defend the gaps in the wall surrounding Jerusalem before it was rebuilt. I remember

Ezekiel 22:30 which says, "I (the Sovereign Lord) looked for someone among them who would build up the wall and stand before me in the gap on behalf of the land." I take this to mean our families as well.

When we are in close relationship with Jesus, we are able to hear His voice as He opens our ears and eyes to what is happening in the spirit world around us and others. He has given us the authority and His blessing to watch over our families. They are being targeted by the devil, who wants to destroy them. If we are not diligent in walking with Jesus, reading His Word, spending time with Him in prayer and knowing Him intimately, we have no right to think He will answer our prayers. With praise and thanksgiving we can come to the One who rules supreme – Jesus Christ – the One who is constantly interceding for us.

He loves us just as we are but it is a relationship with Him that He is seeking from us. When we are in a relationship with another person, they hear us and want the best for us. It is the same with Jesus. He wants us to have the best – not second best. He died on the cross for you and me (WOW!) so we can have life with Him and live it abundantly. This is the life I want – nothing else satisfies.

Allison goes missing

After the attack, and I had returned home, the whole family had some issues to deal with. Our Allison found it difficult to adjust to me telling her what to do as she had been enjoying some freedoms that I was not prepared to continue.

When she was nine years old, she decided to run away from school with two other friends. After receiving a phone call from the school, I set off with my neighbours to drive around the streets looking for her. During our search I came to a bit of an incline on the side of the road with some thick trees. I stopped and looked there but unfortunately I did not get out of the car. If I had, I would have found them. Allison later told me that she had wanted to call out to me but didn't. I drove around for a while, then picked up Chris who took the three of us home while he continued to look with Trevor. With my husband not in Auckland at the time, I was very grateful to have my boys helping in the search.

Back at home, the house started to fill with dear friends who were concerned for Allison's safety. It was late afternoon and there were many people out looking. I felt the need to be alone with my God; I had to get away from people to be with Him. The only place I could think of where no one would follow me was in the shower. There I could sing God's praises to my heart's content. I have no idea what my visitors thought as they heard me singing in the midst of the turmoil but praise Him I did! I came out of the shower feeling refreshed, knowing my God had heard me.

A while later, my neighbour was on his way back to our house when he saw the girls walking up the road. He brought them in and everyone rejoiced. I thanked God for His answer to my prayer and the truth of Proverbs 3:5-6 "Trust in the Lord with all your heart and lean not on your own understanding; in all your ways submit to Him and He will make your paths straight."

We found out later that the girls had planned to spend the night at the primary school nearby but Allison hadn't thought that was a very good idea so she guided them towards our house. Thank you, Lord.

Christopher in Japan

Our eldest son Chris left New Zealand for Japan when he was 21 years old. After working there for a couple of years, he told us he had an opportunity to put on a rock music concert. A scheduled concert organised by other promoters had been cancelled because of a typhoon warning so Chris decided to step in and give it a go.

Never having done anything like this before, he had a lot to learn. About three days before the event, he phoned to say, "Mum, I need 800 people through the gate or I am going down."

"Have you spoken to God about this?" I asked.

"Yeah, yeah, of course I have. Will you pray that I get 800? If I don't, I'll have to find $15,000 just to cover the expenses. I don't have any money! Please pray."

Next day he rang again. "Mum, it's pouring here. I need fine weather – it's an outside venue and if it's raining no one will turn up."

"Yes, I will pray, but are you praying too?"

"Yeah, yeah. I speak to the Big Guy all the time."

The day came and went and I didn't hear from Chris immediately. A couple of days later, having slept for a day or two because he was so tired, he rang to say, "The weather was fine all through the concert but just as I picked up the last bit of rubbish during clean-up at around 3 a.m. the heavens opened."

I said, "Thank you, Lord. But how many did you get through the gate?"

"Amazing," he said, "Eight hundred people came through the gate!"

I realised that was exactly what I'd asked for – no more, no less. Thank you Lord!

Another answer to prayer

Later on during his time there, Chris asked me to go to Japan for a week. He had bought into a language school in Nagasaki with 300 students in various kindergartens and schools. He was part owner with a Japanese man. He told me in the office there was a woman called Mummy who had previously worked in the same premises as an administrator for the Bahá'í community. When the language school took over the premises, Mummy continued working there. She was older than Chris by a few years and she seemed to view him with suspicion because he was a foreigner. Every time he asked her to do something for him, it took her a long time before she did it.

One day while I was having my regular devotional time before Chris got up, I felt that God wanted me to go into the language school and pray through the rooms, cleansing them from Bahá'í influences and dedicating them to God. I woke Chris up, told him what I thought, and he agreed that it was a good idea.

While I was praying, he went to get his dry-cleaning. As I prayed, I placed my hands upon Mummy's empty chair and said, "Lord, you know that Mummy is a hindrance to Chris. If she is not meant to be here, would you please remove her?"

When he got back, I told Chris what I had done. "Oh Mum, but it is so hard to find work in Nagasaki," he said.

"But is she a hindrance to you?" I asked.

"Yes."

"Then we will leave it up to the Lord."

During the day, Chris and I visited the kindergartens where he was teaching. I found it very interesting. He was so much fun and the children just loved him. All they wanted to do was cuddle him, so he had them running all over the place, chasing him. Then he'd fall on the floor and the whole group would pile on top. In all this mayhem he would call out words in English and the children would run and touch the object or do the action he was describing. They loved it and learnt a lot while having fun. Later, we went to a class with older boys – about eight years old – where even more fun was had. In fact, when Chris got married a few years later, one of the boys from this class travelled to New Zealand to be in the wedding party.

After visiting the students, Chris stopped and bought some takeaways for our lunch. When he came back to the car he was running and leaping, looking very, very happy. I asked him what was so exciting and he said, "My co-owner just told me that Mummy handed in her notice two hours ago!"

I immediately prayed and thanked the Lord, asking that Mummy would find another job. Meanwhile, Chris rang his mate and said, "When my mum prays, things really happen!"

The next night I was asked out for dinner by Chris's business partner and his wife. She had been working for a Christian man for years. They were very interested in my prayer about Mummy so I was able to share a little of my story. The gentleman had read the Bible but when I asked him if he would like to become a follower of Jesus, he said, "No, I am a very bad man."

I said, "Jesus accepts us just as we are, and He will help you to change." But it was to no avail.

As we were going down the escalator, the Holy Spirit told me very clearly to ask the man's wife if she would like to ask Jesus into her life. She beamed and said, "Yes please." So right there in the hotel lobby, she became a Christian.

Chris and his girlfriend, Ying (his future wife), picked me up after the dinner and on the way home Ying asked what the power was that surrounded me. I spent the next one and a half hours telling her about Jesus. She didn't become a believer then but did years later.

Freedom from wrong thinking

Trevor also went on his big OE ('overseas experience') when he was 21 years old. He went to the United Kingdom and this is where he met his lovely wife Wendy – a fellow Kiwi from Tauranga.

Before he met Wendy, Trevor had some problems that were affecting his life. He rang me quite often from the boarding house where he was staying in Reading to tell me what was happening. Finally I asked him, "If I could arrange counselling for you from here – and it would be Christian counselling – would you agree to go?"

"Yes," he said.

So I contacted Waverley Abbey College in the UK and asked if they had any male counsellors in Reading? They certainly did, so I gave them Trevor's contact details. Apparently Trevor walked into the first session and said, "You can counsel me, but I don't want prayer." The counsellors agreed to that and after a few weeks, I got a call from Trevor: "Mum, in the counselling session last night something came up."

"It's about me isn't it?" I replied.

He said they had told him not to say anything to me about it. "But," he said, "I know I can talk to you about anything."

It transpired that they had uncovered something that I had already felt in my spirit but didn't understand. From the time Trevor was small, I had made him my buddy instead of being a parent to him. I am a people person; I love company and lots of chatter. Howard, on the other hand, is far more reserved. He has always worked very hard at his job and given just about everything to it. He worked long hours and when he came home he wanted peace and quiet. I tried very hard but I must have driven him mad sometimes. When he walked through the door, out would flow all my frustrations and I would talk all about my day, poor dear. With Trevor, I had someone I could chatter to. Trevor has always been very observant and sensitive to the needs of others around him. This meant that I had someone who would check in on me, give me a cuddle and make sure that I was okay. I always enjoyed our conversations and when he left on his travels, I lost my good mate, and it hurt. I knew though that I had to let him go to become the man God had ordained him to be.

When I got the call from Trevor saying that this was what the counsellors had identified as the problem, I was devastated. I asked for his forgiveness and prayed a prayer to really set him free. Of course, he forgave me. After the conversation, I went to the kitchen, fetched my apron, cut off the ties and posted it to Trevor. It was a symbolic gesture saying that I was grateful he could talk to me about the issue and that I was setting him free. What a difference it made to both of us.

By the way, Howard and I have always had a wonderful relationship. It was my need for constant company that meant I sought someone to talk to and Trevor was an excellent listener. Now that I know Jesus better, I am not as draining on others as I must have been back then. I am very happy in my own company and know the Holy Spirit is my counsellor and friend. I am never alone. "I will ask the Father and He will give you another advocate (counsellor) to help you and be with you forever –the Spirit of truth" (John 14:16-17). At the end of the counselling sessions Trevor asked the men to pray with him. Praise the Lord. Trevor did not come back to Jesus then but he did some time later.

A while later, Trevor rang in tears and explained that he was experiencing a great deal of anxiety and that it was starting to affect his life. He had suffered this anxiety for two years. After some prayer and divine insight we realised he had developed a real fear of rejection and he was worried that the anxiety was going to stop him from enjoying healthy relationships in the future. I prayed for him and told him that I firmly believed God would heal the hurt and that he would be very happily married one day (and of course now he is). Afterwards, I thought of something and called him back. I asked him to go and pray through his room, invite the Holy Spirit to dwell there and to cast out anything that might have remained from previous tenants. I then prayed blessings upon Trevor. The sound of deliverance that came over the phone was wonderful. I thanked God for giving me amazing insight to help our son on his journey.

CHAPTER SEVEN

Miracles of Grace and Protection

Howard took on a new role which meant that he was commuting to Nelson during the week and coming home at the weekends. One Friday evening before Christmas he had a function to attend so he stayed in Nelson for the night. Allison was at her friend's place and I was at home alone.

At about 2 a.m. I was awake and couldn't sleep so I decided to fill in the time with prayer. The light above me suddenly came on and then went off. I realised there must be somebody in my house. I got out of bed, walked past the phone, had a look down the hallway and saw the door in the passage which I had left open was shut. A righteous anger welled up inside me. How dare anyone come into my house! I stormed down the passage, turning on the lights, then into the kitchen and there was the ranch slider partly open.

Instead of ringing the police I rang my friend Marian and asked her to stay on the phone while I looked around the house. The intruder had taken the television, two bottles of wine from under the Christmas tree and the video remote but not the video player.

"Aren't you supposed to be ringing the police?" asked Marian. I told her I would and she said she was coming around. The police were ready to send someone straightaway but I told them I didn't believe the burglar was still in the house and that I would be okay as I had a friend coming to sit with me. They asked if I wanted victim support, which I declined. They told me they would come again in the morning to take fingerprints.

Marian arrived and we decided to go through the house to make certain the burglar wasn't still there. When we got back to the lounge, we sat down and I prayed. I asked the Lord to cleanse the house again. I prayed that nothing from the intruder would remain, that he would be caught, he would confess to the burglary and Howard and I would get our things back. Marian then went home and I slept well.

Unfortunately, I forgot to tell Howard what had happened. The next morning, he arrived home to find a police car in the drive. He came steaming through the house and into the dining room where I was talking to the police officer. Oh dear, the look on Howard's face! "I'm okay," I said, "Everything is okay." Then I had to explain. When I had finished he said, "You are coming to Nelson!" Allison and I shifted south early the next year and we lived there for 18 months with Howard.

Two weeks after Christmas we had a call from a very excited police constable at about 10:30 p.m. She told us that they had the man who had burgled our house. He had confessed to the burglary and they had our things. God is amazing!

A ball paused in mid-air

I was playing golf with Howard one morning. We had finished the first nine. On the second nine, one of the tees had a border of pine trees and a pond behind the trees. We had been following four men, one of whom was hitting his ball all over the place. When we walked up to wait our turn, Howard said to me, "Stand here behind this tree." He then went over to the pond to see if he could find any lost balls (a part-time hobby of his).

For some reason, I stepped out from the safety of the trees. Sure enough, the chap who had been hitting all over the place took his shot and instead of travelling straight down the fairway, the ball flew to the left and straight at me. When I heard the men yell, "Fore!" I turned my head to see that the ball had stopped in mid-flight on the right side of my head, next to my ear. I could have reached up and taken it in my hand. Instead, I ducked my head forward and the ball parted the back of my hair as it whooshed past me and landed some distance away.

I looked over at the men, who were standing by the tee with their mouths open. Then they all started talking at once. They decided to call it a day and quickly walked off the course. I wish I had asked them what they thought of this miracle. I would have told them about my God. Meanwhile, my beloved came back and we continued on with our game. I told him that I had nearly been hit by a ball. "I told you to stay behind the trees!" he said.

"Yes darling, I will next time!"

Sharks

In the summer months Howard and I used to go fishing on our boat in the Hauraki Gulf. We were out one day on the south side of Tiritiri Matangi Island in the channel. We had no bites, not even a nibble. Howard suggested we go further out to a group of islands called The Noises – usually a good fishing spot. I agreed but wanted to have a swim before we set off.

I dived over the side and as I came to the surface, the still small voice inside me said, "What about the sharks?" I have never worried about that sort of thing before but this time I definitely felt uncomfortable so I swam around to the back of the boat and hung onto the ladder. Still feeling very uncomfortable, I climbed on board. No sooner had we started off than we motored through a school of hammerhead sharks sunning themselves on top of the water. There was a mass of them, too many to count or guess the number. As we drove through, the ones in our path dived but the rest just kept sunning themselves. I was certainly praising my God that day – and yes, I still swim while out in the deep and I love it!

God's guidance

As my friend Marian and I were driving to Pauanui for a much-needed break, we rounded a corner and saw a place that looked good for lunch. As we were about to pay for our food, I looked up at the person serving us and recognised her from my past. I spoke her name and she remembered me. She said she would come over and talk when she had finished serving.

It turned out that she was the owner of the place so we caught up on news and then she shared with me about her sister who was dying of cancer. I said I could see her pain and would she like us to pray for her? "Yes please," she said, "I'll see if I can get away for a few moments." She took us over to her house across a courtyard and as we were walking there, the Lord said one word to me: "Salvation."

When we'd sat down I prayed for her and then said, "Have you ever asked Jesus into your heart?" She said she hadn't. She had a friend who was a Christian and who had spoken to her about Christ before. I asked her if she would like to commit her life to Jesus now.

"Yes," she said, and so I led her in a prayer. As we were leaving I gave her a Living Bible which had belonged to my son Trevor. Marian and I left there singing the praises of our God. The woman rang me later to tell me her sister had passed away and that she would like me to come to the funeral.

A tradesman's defining moment

We needed our lounge suite sprayed with fabric protector and the man who came to do the work commented on my daily devotional *Word for Today* that was sitting on the chest of drawers. So I asked him if he also had the book. "Yes," he said, "but I find it hard to read."

I asked if he read the Bible on a regular basis and he said he used to but found it hard going now and had stopped. I encouraged him to pick it up again as it would help him in his daily work. We talked about where he went to church and what he liked to do. Motorbikes were his passion. I asked if he was married and he said he was; his wife went to church more often than he did. I then felt the Holy Spirit put into my mind the book *Wild at Heart* by John Eldredge and I offered it to him to read. He was concerned about how he would return it to me so I suggested he could put it in my mail box when he'd finished with it. Some time went by until, out of the blue, I got a call from a woman who said she used to come to a Bible study at my house in Forrest Hill. I told her I was sorry, I couldn't remember her. Then she told me her story:

"For a couple of months now, I've watched my husband come home from work, walk straight through the door, sit down with a book, and read and read. He hasn't done anything like that for a long time but he couldn't put this book down. Yesterday I found the book – it was called *Wild at Heart* – and there was your name in the front. When he came home I told him I had looked at it and I knew you. Last night we had a good long discussion about our lives and how unhappy he had been for a long time – not with me, but where his life was heading."

The book had put a whole new perspective into his life. The couple was now thinking of shifting south to Invercargill to live in the wide open spaces where he could do the things he had wanted to do all his life. She said it was a huge step but she knew it was the right one and was looking forward to it. She thanked me so much for being obedient to what the Holy Spirit had asked me to do. I didn't hear from them again but the book arrived back in my letter box not long after that.

Instant interpretation

After Howard retired we travelled to Europe for three months. We hired a campervan and drove 12,000 kilometres around the continent. It was wonderful to be able to see all the cities and countries I had always longed to see. On one occasion when we were travelling in Italy I accidentally directed us north instead of south. The night set in and still we travelled on until finally we stopped at a bar to ask for directions and find out if we could stay the night in their car park. The establishment was run by an older gentleman and his son who was about 60 years old. I had a lot of fun getting them to understand me but they showed me on the map where we were, which of course was not where we were supposed to be. We laughed together and yes, they understood that we wanted to stay the night. Then all of a sudden the older gentleman said in perfect English, "You need to go and put your head down."

I replied, "Yes I do, thank you so much."

It wasn't until I was in bed in our campervan that I realised what had just taken place. This dear soul couldn't understand me or I him and yet the Lord interpreted what he said, as clear and as distinct as if he were speaking perfect English. Of course, after I realised this I was so excited I couldn't sleep. This is just one of the many wonderful memories I have of our travels.

Howard and Trixie marry in 1966.

Trixie's sister, Meriel, three days before she died.

Woman Hurled Over Bridge Railing

By DAVID BISHOP

A 70-year-old woman watched in horror yesterday as her daughter was thrown from a central Auckland bridge and fell about six metres on to a tarsealed carpark.

Mrs Trixie Elaine Jellie, of Forrest Hill, suffered head injuries, a broken pelvis and a broken leg after being hurled from the Myers Lane overbridge on Mayoral Drive, close to Queen St.

The 42-year-old mother and housewife is in the critical care unit of Auckland Hospital. Her condition was described last night as serious but stable.

Detective Inspector Mike Crawford, of the Auckland police, said the victim had been shopping in town with her 70-year-old mother.

At 10.30 am the pair returned to their car, which was parked in Mayoral Drive.

Mrs Jellie's mother got into the front passenger seat.

Struggle

"The victim heard someone call out to her. She turned and saw a man standing by the railing at the edge of the bridge. He came over to her and put her in a headlock," said Detective Inspector Crawford.

"The man dragged her over to the rail and quite a struggle ensued. The victim was beaten about the head during the struggle and was dragged partially over the railing.

"Her attacker then threw her over the rail and off the bridge."

Detective Inspector Crawford said all this happened as Mrs Jellie's mother watched, horror-struck. The man and Mrs Jellie did not know each other, he said.

Two policemen who were waiting for the lights to change at the nearby intersections of Greys Ave and Mayoral Drive saw the pair struggling.

Scuffle

Constable Mario DiLeva was sitting in the passenger seat of the marked patrol

Police at the spot where Mrs Jellie landed. CENTRE: The Myers Lane overbridge where the attack took place, and, at right, Constable Siddell (left) and Constable DiLeva at the scene

Press clippings about the bridge attack.

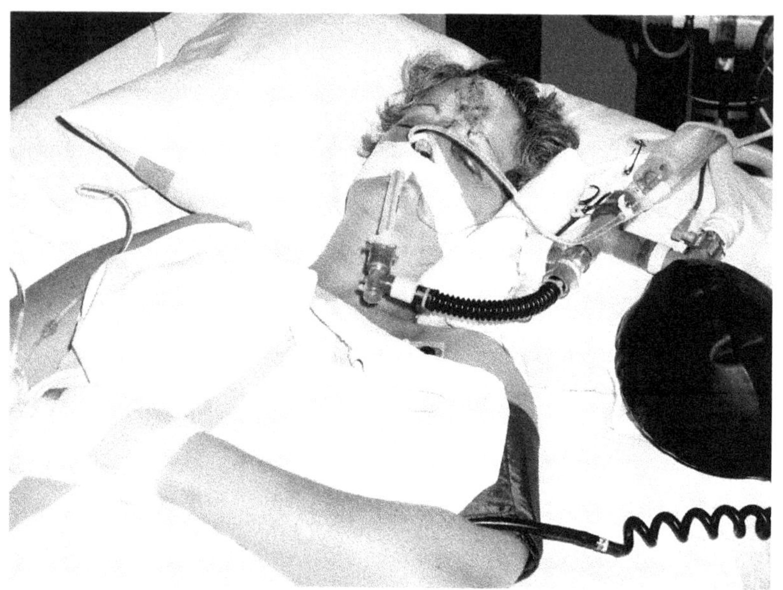

Top: Trixie in ICU after the attack. Bottom: Reading a special card from Trixie's Bible In Schools class with Allison.

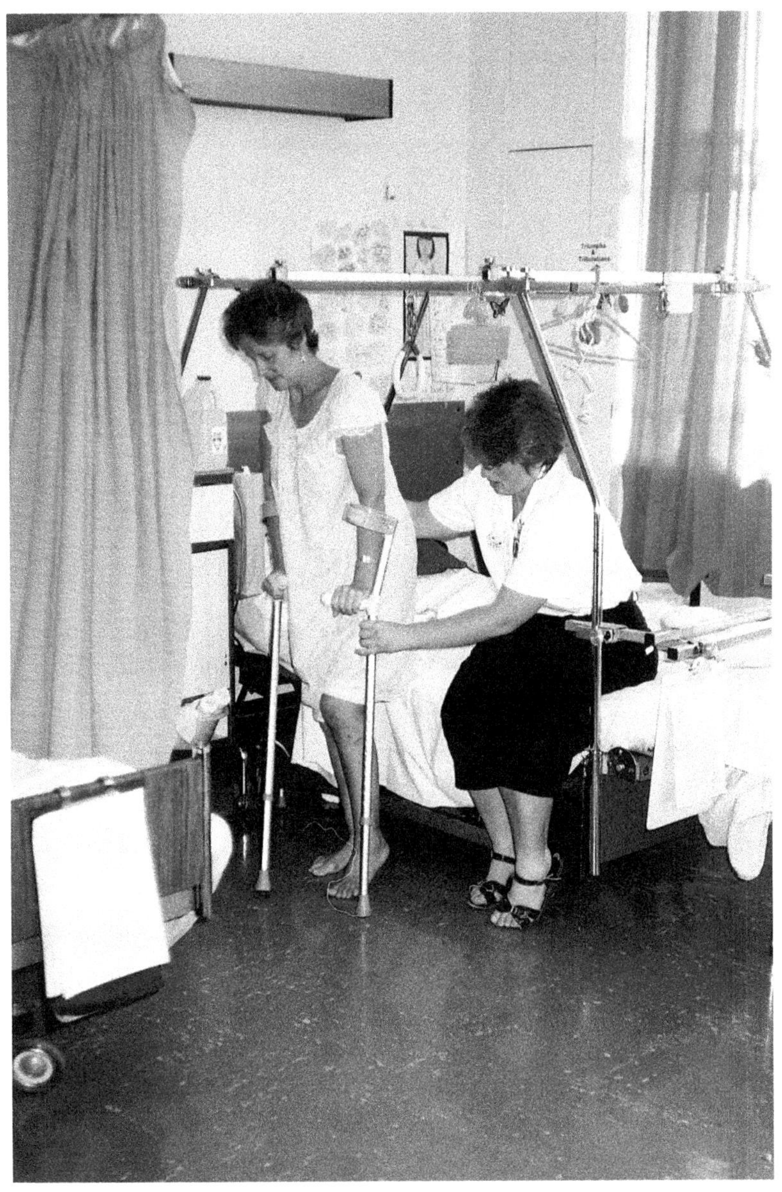

Trixie getting back up on her feet.

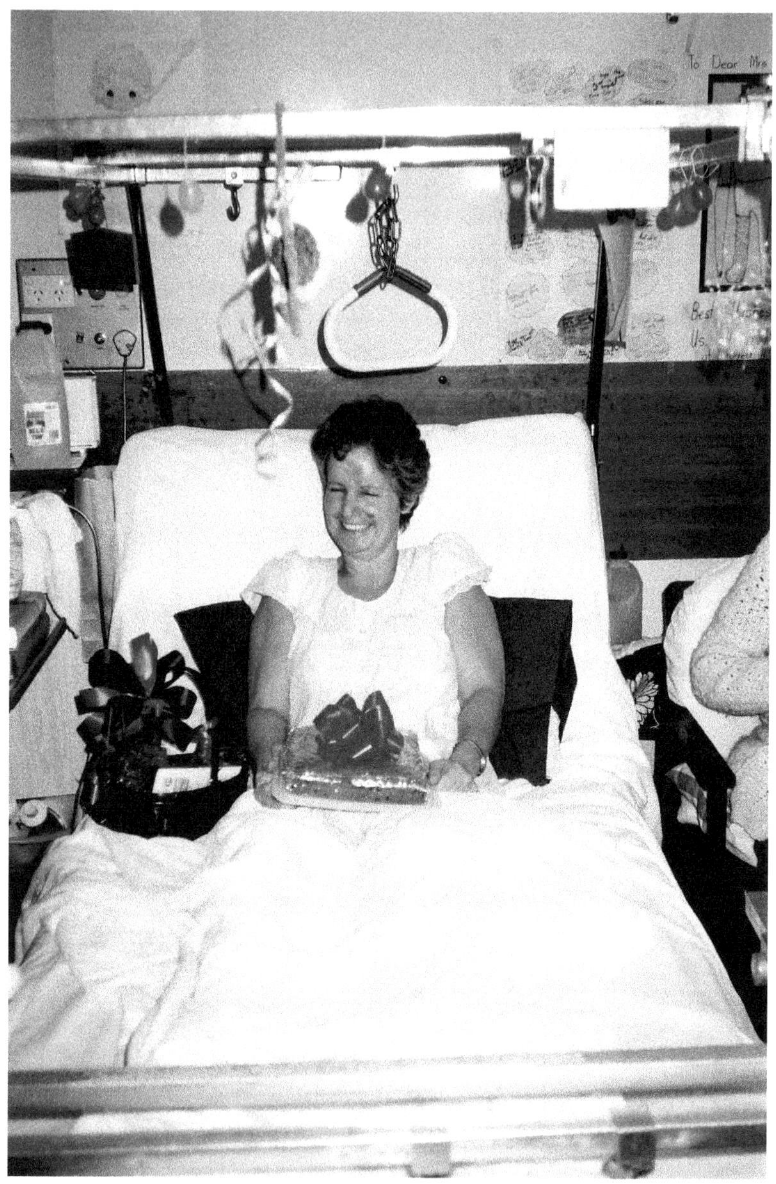

Trixie, the day before leaving hospital, celebrating the milestone in her recovery.

A portrait of the Jellie family taken in 1993.

Trixie leaping from a plane for her 60th birthday.

Revisiting the scene of the attack in 2017.

Howard and Trixie, 2017.

CHAPTER EIGHT

Learning to Claim Healing

Twelve years after the attack, when I was living in Nelson, a person from ACC asked me if I'd suffered brain damage. I said I had no idea. In those days, hospitals simply dealt with the injuries they could see. ACC arranged for a psychiatrist to come to my home and test me. He told me that I did in fact have brain damage.

It really is terrible how words can dictate the way we think and cause us to behave. I started making excuses for the things I forgot. Up to this point, I had always relied upon the Holy Spirit. Any time I couldn't remember something, I countered it by saying, "Thank you Lord for my retentive memory" and whatever it was would pop into my mind. However, after receiving this diagnosis I stopped proclaiming this prayer of faith. Worse still, I spoke out the negative over my life. I latched onto the negative instead of thanking the Lord and declaring I was healed. Negativity can grab hold of us and strangle the very life out of us, until we realise the damaging effect it is having on our lives. I truly believe though that by trusting in God and the power of His Holy Spirit, and by speaking positively, we can overcome anything. "Do not be anxious about anything, but in every situation, by prayer and petition, with thanksgiving, present your requests to God. And the peace of God, which transcends all understanding, will guard your hearts and your minds in Christ Jesus" (Philippians 4:6-7).

Menopause

When I first started to get hot flushes, I put up with the inconvenience until one day I thought: "Where does it say in the Bible that I have to suffer this?" Once again, I took the authority given to me by Jesus and spoke out those same words, adding, "In the name of Jesus, stop this nonsense immediately." And it stopped!

I do understand that there are some women who need help in this area. For me, though, I believed this was what God wanted me to do and He honoured my faith. God says in His Word: "Truly I tell you, unless you change and become like little children, you will never enter the kingdom of heaven. Therefore, whoever takes the lowly position of this child is the greatest in the kingdom of heaven" (Matthew 18:3-4). When you share something with a child, there is no question for them that what you're saying is true. You said it, they trust you, and so to them it is true. This is exactly how it is when I read the Bible. I don't question whether it is true; I simply believe it, speak it out and wait for God to move. It is the very life to our bodies and all we have to do is speak it out. "All Scripture is God-breathed and is useful for teaching, rebuking, correcting and training in righteousness, so that the servant of God may be thoroughly equipped for every good work" (2 Timothy 3:16-17). What an amazing God to give us such a powerful tool for us to use.

Bowel cancer

When we arrived home from our travels in Europe, Howard's old firm asked us to go to Wales for nine months to oversee a job there. We thought this opportunity sounded pretty good. Before we left we decided to visit our son and daughter-in-law in Japan. I had not been well the week before we went but the doctor had given me some tablets. It helped for a day or two but I began to get terrible pain in my abdomen, which I would best describe as being in labour. We were in Japan for a week and the days seemed to drag. I just wanted to come home and rang to ask Allison to make an appointment with my doctor on the day we arrived back in Auckland.

Back home, I was sent for an X-ray which showed a lot of inflammation and explained why I was in so much pain. By this time it was about 5.30 p.m. The doctor said I could spend the night at home but if the pain got too bad, I was to go to the hospital. I went in later that evening. In the morning a specialist admitted me after saying he could feel a lump. After I had been in hospital for about 10 days, the specialist performed a colonoscopy which revealed a tumour. He showed us the picture of the growth but the situation still did not register with me. He patiently waited for it to sink in.

I finally said to him, "Are you telling me I have the Big C?"

"Yes, I am sorry, that is right." It was cancer. He left us to ponder this news. I was scheduled to be operated on the next morning. When I asked him how long he thought I might have had the tumour, he said, "About two years."

After the operation I was told I needed to have chemotherapy. Obviously this was not my first choice and my prayer was for God to heal me without this treatment. I would have loved Him to heal me instantly but through the journey of chemotherapy, I met so many wonderful people and was able to share the gospel with them. God can use any situation for His glory, if we let Him.

Chemo

I was told I would need chemotherapy once a week for seven months. This was a bitter pill to swallow. I would like you to know that through all these trials there were times when I struggled and lost my joy. I had times of crying out to God and telling Him how hard things were but He would always come back with the assurance that He would always be with me. I knew I could trust and rely on Him. I clung to His promise in Isaiah 41:10 "Do not fear, for I am with you; do not be dismayed, for I am your God. I will strengthen you and help you; I will uphold you with my righteous right hand."

I praise my God that He is always faithful and He always goes before us. Earlier in the year, we had bought a holiday home north of Auckland. It needed a lot of work throughout but it was a dream come true to have a bach near the beach. We had made a start on this and I was diagnosed about five months later. I received my chemo dose every Friday and afterwards we would travel up north for the week, where Howard pottered around while I rested. He was transforming a very run-down house into a lovely holiday home for the whole family to enjoy. God's provision is always perfect. I came through the seven months of treatment very well – I grew quite thin but I didn't lose my hair.

Blood clots

Near the end of the chemotherapy treatment I started to experience pain just below my rib cage on the left. It was a nuisance to me but I carried on because I thought it was probably something I'd eaten. On Howard's birthday, we went out for dinner with Allison, Karl and their children.

Allison had been telling me all day that I should have the pain checked out. When we got home I went upstairs to bed. Suddenly the pain shifted from under my rib cage to my left shoulder. It was more intense – and that really got my attention. I rang oncology and they advised me to go to the emergency department at Auckland Hospital. The doctor on duty wasn't sure what the problem was but he admitted me for the night. The next morning they did tests, including a CT scan.

In the ward there were a lot of people coming and going but I remember one woman in particular who had been in there numerous times. She said the doctors had done all they could for her. I prayed for her and she gave me her phone number. I rang a few weeks later but was told she had passed away. She had told me she used to attend a Baptist church in Henderson; I am hoping I will see her again in heaven.

Later that day, the nurses started injecting me with a blood thinner called Clexane, the treatment for the blood clots they had discovered in the scan. The doctor had been to see me but he didn't say what was wrong, just that they would start the injections and that the nurses would show me how to inject myself at home. At this time we accepted that doctors knew what they were doing and never questioned anything. Howard and I have now learnt that it is okay and actually quite important to ask questions and understand what is going on.

The doctor finally said I could go home and told me not to do anything strenuous. A haematology appointment in two weeks' time was made for me. I still didn't question what was happening and still hadn't been told that I had clots. It sounds silly – and it would have been so simple to ask – but I believed the doctors would tell me if it was anything serious and because nothing was mentioned specifically, I thought everything was fine. It wasn't until the haematology appointment a fortnight later that the doctor remarked how lucky I was to be alive after having large blood clots in both lungs. My husband paled and it's fair to say we were both taken aback.

Migraines

I have suffered from horrible migraines since I was a teenager. I've swallowed heaps of tablets, had injections, experienced all the symptoms, and been out of it for three days at a time while I slowly got back on my feet.

One day I was reading the Bible when I questioned the Lord about our bodies being the temple of God. I said, "Lord, every man-made temple has the holy of holies in it and if I am the temple of God, I must have a holy of holies within me. If this is the case, then, just like the temple of old, no evil can come into the holy of holies." I sensed the presence of the Lord all around me so I then said, "Lord, if I am understanding you correctly, I need confirmation to know that it is you who is revealing this to me."

A couple of days later I was reading the book *Right People, Right Place, Right Plan* by Jentezen Franklin. Here was my confirmation because the book was saying the very thing I had asked the Lord about. I was so excited, I couldn't believe my eyes! It wasn't long before I heard the same truth from the pulpit at my church, City Impact Church on the North Shore. It is wonderful to be in a church that teaches from the Word of God in such depth. God reveals different things to different people. The closer you come to know Him, the more He reveals Himself through His Word.

After this revelation I decided to call on the name of Jesus, praise Him for who He is, quote Scripture, and not take any pills for the migraines. Well, sometimes it would take a while for the lights to subside, other times it would happen more quickly but whatever happened, I realised that God would do it in His way. I then started getting migraines in the middle of the night or at any time during the day. I believed this was the work of Satan trying to make me cave in. When we stand up and choose to fight, the devil will try to come in and make us buckle. At these times, I reminded myself of how Jesus died for me on the cross and rose again to give me new life, including the power to overcome sickness. Most of the time, I would overcome because God says in the Bible that the battle is His and the victory is ours. At other times I did cave in – especially if I was in the company of people who wouldn't understand if I started quoting Scripture or I was tired in mind and body. I am not proud of this but it has been a time of learning.

During one holiday up north, I had five migraines in the space of four days. I started out strong but then buckled under the strain.

I had stopped relying on Jesus. I rang my mentor, Jean, who told me she had been on her way to her couch to pray when the Holy Spirit gave her a revelation. She believed that I was suffering the effects of a curse. I knew she was right so I claimed the authority of Jesus and sent the curse packing. "Like a fluttering sparrow or a darting swallow, an undeserved curse does not come to rest" (Proverbs 26:2).

I had been putting up with these horrible migraines and not asking the Holy Spirit about the source. Now I had the knowledge and power to overcome. I didn't necessarily believe someone had intentionally cursed me; it could just be the negative words that they were speaking about me. This was a difficult lesson and one I am still working on now.

The wrong pills

I had been suffering heart flutters for years. My daughter-in-law suggested I should go to see a specialist. He recommended that I should try a very low dose of Flecainide. About four years later, I started noticing I was getting slower but I put it down to getting old before my time because of what my body had endured over the years. My poor husband could see I was not as full of life as I used to be. He encouraged me to exercise. I tried going to a gym but that made me even more tired. Everything I did seemed to make me tired. It was so unlike me.

One day I had a terrible experience. I was in the shower when I felt the pressure building up in my head. My heart was racing and the pain in my head was unlike anything I had experienced before. I really thought I was dying. After a while it subsided but I was exhausted and very weak for the rest of the day. It took a few days before I told my beloved. After everything I have been through, I wasn't keen to give him anything new to worry about. When it happened a second time, I decided to 'fess up.

We thought I should go to the doctor but before I could get there I had another attack, then a fourth at church one Sunday. This one wasn't as bad as the others but again it left me with no energy. A few days later there was a pain under my rib cage on the left. It reminded me of when I'd had the blood clots in my lungs. Back to the hospital we went but they couldn't find anything wrong. A week or so later I had another trip to hospital and stayed overnight this time but again, the doctors found nothing that would explain the symptoms.

I went to my doctor and he suggested I go back to the specialist, which I did. I was given a treadmill test along with a raft of blood tests and this time the readings from my heart showed something that absolutely shocked him. He told me he didn't know why I was experiencing these attacks but that I should go home and rest. At the end of the week he rang to say: "Stop the Flecainide – the results from your blood tests show you have Flecainide toxicity."

It's not normally advisable to just stop taking a heart pill like that and the change sent me to bed for about two weeks, unable to do anything. We asked for a second opinion. This doctor said he didn't understand why I had been put onto Flecainide in the first place as my original symptoms were typical of what 80 percent of the population experiences with their hearts. It took me some time to come to grips with what I had gone through in the last four years. Yes, there was anger; yes, there was unforgiveness in me, which I had to bring before the Lord.

After a time, the specialist chose to put a heart monitor in my chest wall. Not a pacemaker – just a monitor to see what my heart is doing. It will stay there for about three years. As yet, it hasn't shown anything major. I believe it won't, as I stand on the Word of my God. He is my healer and deliverer in whom I trust.

A sobering experience

Pastor Tim Hall from Australia came to minister healing at our church one Sunday morning. As he prayed, he asked people to place their hands upon areas of their bodies that needed healing. I did this because I had just spent a month in the South Island, driving around in pain while sitting for long periods of time. Each time I sat in the car, the pain would immediately start.

I believed I was healed instantly. Pastor Tim then asked people to come to the front of the church to share how they had been healed. I went forward but I put aside the healing I had just received and talked instead about the attempted murder and the smashed pelvis I had suffered.

These were the days when I wasn't waiting on God to promote me. He had shown me I would be sharing my story with many people and for a number of years I had had many opportunities. But lately the invitations to speak had stopped. I believe this was because God knew what the next few years would bring and I really don't think I could have coped with speaking engagements on top of my extreme tiredness. At the time, however, I was trying to push myself forward instead of waiting on the Lord. And that was the mistake I made that Sunday morning.

Pastor Tim asked me up on stage with the others to share. When he asked me what I had received healing for and why, I looked at Pastor Peter Mortlock. In that instant, it was as if I received a bolt of lightning from Peter's eyes to mine. I felt the Holy Spirit was speaking through him to me; He knew my motives weren't pure. After this experience, I had to submit afresh to Jesus and let Him make the changes within me. This didn't happen overnight but after a period of a few years I feel I am slowly getting to grips with this ego of mine. "When pride comes, then comes disgrace, but with humility comes wisdom" (Proverbs 11:2).

Breast cancer

Late in November 2014 I was upstairs praying one day. I thought I would get into the shower and praise my God as that's how I love to relax. As I was about to climb in, I glanced in the mirror and my eyes zoomed onto my right breast – almost like a camera. I thought, "This doesn't look right." The areola (the ring around the nipple) wasn't round anymore and I knew something wasn't right. It was a Friday, so I decided I wouldn't say anything until I could see the doctor on Monday.

So off I went again to the doctor, who agreed it didn't look right and sent me off to a breast clinic. A routine mammogram a few months earlier had shown nothing out of the ordinary and the one they took this day was the same. I also had an ultrasound which showed something that the doctor thought was significant enough for a biopsy. The next week I was informed I had a very high grade cancer. Fortunately, it was still in the milk duct and had not become invasive.

We had heard that New Zealand is world class in breast cancer treatment. The public health system had been excellent when I had bowel cancer so we decided to change from having a private specialist. The day we saw our doctor was a Tuesday, two weeks before Christmas. The same day, North Shore Hospital rang and made an appointment for the following Tuesday. The surgeon we spoke to at the hospital arranged an operation for Thursday of that same week. After the operation, I went to see the surgeon two days before Christmas. She told me I would be having more surgery on 29 January 2015 to make sure they had removed all the cancer cells. After that it would be up to me to decide whether or not to have radiotherapy.

Did I feel like screaming? Yes, especially after speaking to the oncologist and hearing about the radiation. I didn't want this for my body. I didn't understand why I had to go through something else, especially when the surgeon said she felt there wouldn't be any cancer remaining after the second surgery. She told me it was my choice. Howard and I thought it through and decided to go ahead with radiotherapy. I truly believe it was Jesus who showed me the difference in my breast that day and it was He who arranged everything so quickly. I really had to trust Him to get me through and I am so grateful to Dr Eva at North Shore Hospital for adding me to her very busy schedule just before Christmas.

When the day for radiotherapy arrived, I had such a heavy heart. I had been up since 4:30 a.m., talking to the Lord and reading the Bible. I held onto Philippians 4:13 "I can do all this through him who gives me strength."

Confronted by God

Pastor Norm McLeod from Gisborne was preaching at our church one morning. When he asked people to raise their hands in response to the call for salvation, I heard Jesus say to me, "You are not happy with the way your life has gone, are you?"

I was very happy with my marriage and family and I knew God wasn't referring to that. I instantly knew He meant the attack and all the medical things that had taken place over the last few years. I replied, "No Lord, it has been pretty hard."

He then said, "Will you reaffirm your love for me by raising your hand in this altar call?"

The tears started to fall and big sobs came from deep within me as I lifted my hand. It was just God and me. I forgot everything around me and just bathed in His love as I surrendered my life anew to my God in whom I trust. I had no idea that I had buried all these feelings within me as He brought each one to the surface and I asked forgiveness; they surely had been stopping the flow of the Holy Spirit in my life.

I praise God that He always knows everything about me. As

Psalm 139:2-4 says, "You know when I sit and when I rise; you perceive my thoughts from afar. You discern my going out and my lying down; you are familiar with all my ways. Before a word is on my tongue you, Lord, know it completely."

When I became aware again of what was happening around me, I opened my eyes to find a lovely young lady asking me if I would like to go to the front of the church. I thanked her and said I had been in the church for a long time and that I had been spending time with Jesus. I noticed Pastor Norm looking at me and probably wondering why I wasn't going to the front but I knew I had just been with Jesus and that's all I needed. I was sitting with friends who knew something was going on but no one asked about it, although I would have told them if they had asked. I walked out that morning a changed person. Every encounter I have had with my Jesus has changed me as I draw closer to Him. Oh how I love Him, He is my all!

CHAPTER NINE

God's Grace in Action

I had a Papua New Guinean friend named Anna. We met at Aglow and quickly became firm friends. Anna had been in remission from lung cancer for some years when I met her. Unfortunately it came back and she became very sick as it spread to her throat as well as other parts of her body. Her illness didn't stop her witnessing though. No matter where she was, no matter who she was with, she would talk about Jesus. I miss her very much but I know she is in heaven now and in no pain, and that I will see her again.

When I went to see Anna in the hospice one evening, she said she missed having hugs so I climbed up onto her bed and just lay there, cuddling her. It was very special. The day after Anna passed away, I rang her sister and asked if she would like to go out for a coffee. The pastoral care couple who had looked after Anna and her family encouraged Anna's sister to come with me. So I picked her up, bought coffee and took her to Mt Victoria in Devonport.

As we sat in the car with our takeaway coffee looking at the view, I asked her how she was. She said she was struggling and that there were some things she didn't agree with about how the funeral was to be conducted. We discussed her concerns and I believe I was able to help her see what Anna's wishes were. I asked if I could talk about Jesus and how much Anna loved Him. I knew she had been very against anything to do with Jesus but had witnessed His love through the pastoral care couple. Anna's daughter had become a Christian a few days before and now sitting here with Anna's sister, I was able to ask her if she would like to commit her life to Jesus. Praise the Lord she said "yes" and I was able to introduce her to the Lord right there in the car. I then asked her if she had heard Anna praying in a different language. "Yes," she said, so I explained to her about being baptised in the Holy Spirit and asked if she would like to ask the Holy Spirit to do this for her? "Yes!" So I prayed and out from her mouth came a heavenly language. I asked her if it was different from any Papua New Guinean language she knew and she confirmed she had never heard it before. What a joy it was to be used by God to reach my beautiful friend's sister.

I took her back home and said I would see her at the funeral. There, she looked and spoke very much like a different person. She was smiling and gave me such a big hug. I asked the pastoral care person if she had noticed anything different about Anna's sister. She said she had, so I shared what God had done at Mt Victoria. We both praised and thanked our God.

The mother of a visiting pastor

Much to my delight, I was given the opportunity to share my story on Shine TV. A few years later, I arrived at church to be told that a pastor from the South Island had come to Auckland with his family and brought his mother with them. She wanted to talk to me because she had seen me on TV. After the service, I was introduced to her and she told me she had been through many things in her life, just as I had, so she felt she could talk to me. She said that she had heard many invitations to become a Christian but had never responded publicly. I asked her if she had ever made a commitment to follow Jesus. She said "no", so I asked her if she would like me to pray with her and introduce her to Him. "Yes please," she said. So I did. We hugged and kissed – she was so happy. The Bible tells us that heaven rejoices when even one person turns to God. What a special moment it was.

Newspaper witness

I had been asked to share my story at an Aglow meeting. I had spoken about it a couple of times before and on this occasion the *North Shore Times* community newspaper asked if they could interview me before the meeting. I asked Howard what he thought but he said only I could make the decision. I felt I needed to be alone with God and find out what He wanted me to do.

Allison and her two children were going to climb North Head, the old naval gun emplacement in Devonport, and they asked if I would like to come too. When we arrived, they gave me some time to myself so I sat on the rock wall in front of the big old gun with my Bible, seeking God. As I sat there and read I felt His presence all about me. When I looked out across the harbour to the Bean Rock lighthouse, I felt God saying, "I want you to be my shining light to draw people to me," but also that I was not to do the interview. In my mind's eye I saw the light shining out into the darkness from Bean Rock. I had such joy and peace – I knew I had heard from my God.

Just then, Allison and the children arrived. She looked at me and said, "You've got your answer haven't you!" We all went for a walk and Nana showed her little darlings the proper way to do roly-polies down a grassy slope.

A few days later I got a call from the *North Shore Times* woman who asked me if she could come and interview me before the day of the Aglow meeting. I said I didn't think that would be a good idea. She explained that a lot more people would come to hear me if the interview appeared in the paper beforehand. I told her I believed God would bring along the people who needed to hear what I had to say.

On the day I was to speak, the reporter came up to me before the meeting and introduced herself. What a lovely young woman she was. Interestingly, most of the Aglow regulars did not come that day. Five minutes before we started, there were only a few people in the audience but they soon started coming in until the place was virtually full. The Aglow president had advertised the topic as 'When Life is Tough'. I believe this title spoke to the hearts of the women and this is what drew them.

I received a letter from the young reporter afterwards, saying that meeting was her last job as she was heading overseas that very week. She wished me well and said I had given her a lot to think about. I praise God for the seeds sown in her life and ask God to bring them to fruition.

We sow seeds, God waters them

As God's children, we can sow a word, which is like a seed, into a hungry heart and God the gardener will water it, bringing people into that person's life who will help them find Jesus. They then have the choice to accept Jesus or walk away.

I was down at the beach on a cold, windy day in the middle of winter. Two young men were trying to get their windsurfer up and running while a woman with a little boy standing beside her and a very new little baby in her arms watched them.

I was collecting bits and pieces for my hobby of making doves, fish and birds out of shells. I wasn't far away when one of the young men started shouting a horrible four-letter word again and again at the top of his voice while he strode back and forth. My goodness, he was angry! The young woman walked along the beach to find shelter from the wind behind the sand dunes while he carried on.

I stood there and just looked at him for a while, then went back to searching for shells. I said to the Lord, "Lord, if you want me to talk to him, you will have to bring him to me as I'm not going to approach him."

After a while, I saw his feet in front of me. I looked up and he said, "I just want to apologise for my bad language."

Silently I prayed to the Holy Spirit: "Your words, not mine." Then I asked, "Did the bad language do it?"

He looked at me with wide eyes. "No," he said.

"Did the two-year-old's tantrum do it?"

"No," he said, looking like something had just hit him.

"Well, I know someone who gives perfect peace, a peace that surpasses all understanding and His name is Jesus Christ, the Son of God. I know this because I know Him personally." I told him a little bit about what Jesus meant in my life and how He had died on the cross for every one of us.

"This is amazing," he said. "Last night I called out for help." He had been drinking and knew that his drinking was affecting him and his behaviour.

"I am the answer to your prayer," I replied. "This is a divine encounter. God has been calling you for a long time, hasn't He?"

"Yes," he said. "I tried going to a Mormon church for two years when I was 21 but I didn't find what I was looking for." We talked for a little while longer. Then he confessed, "I also said last night that I would stop drinking because it makes me lazy."

I encouraged him to give up alcohol and then asked him where he lived.

"North of Kamo," he said. I told him about the church there where Trevor knows the pastor.

"Turn around and look at your friends," I said. "Is that your wife?"

"Yes."

"And your little boy?"

"Yes."

"Is that how you want him to grow up? Children learn by example – are you being a good example?"

"No." We must have been talking for about 20 minutes. He then pointed out the other man who was a bit further down the beach; it was his brother-in-law whose marriage had just broken up. I made the comment, "He needs Jesus too."

"Yes he does," the young man said.

I asked him if he would like to ask Jesus into his heart now. "Oh that is a big one, I will have to think on that," he replied. So I encouraged him not to leave it too long, especially after that day! I gave him my phone number when we parted company. I haven't heard from him but I thank the Lord that He will water the seeds that I was privileged to plant in that young man's heart.

Giving away a crockpot

I was helping my mentor Jean sort out her kitchen because she was moving house. She had a crockpot to either donate to a hospice or give away. I took it with me in the boot of my car. As I arrived at the supermarket I asked the Lord to show me if there was someone He wanted me to give it to. While fetching a trolley, though, I jumped the gun and asked a woman if she would like the crockpot.

"No, thanks," she said. Oh dear, I hadn't waited for the Lord's prompting. So I whispered a quick apology to Him and went inside to do my shopping.

Standing in the queue at the checkout, I saw a man paying for his items and I knew he was the one. As he was going out the door I said, "Excuse me, but do you have a crockpot?"

"No," he said.

"Would you like one? I have one to give away."

"Yes," was his stunned reply. I told him where my car was and went back to get my groceries. He was waiting for me by my car and as soon as I walked up, he shook my hand and said, "Thank you, thank you so much. I am a single dad with three children – my wife died three years ago. My children will be very happy to have something else to help with the meals."

I took out a church card and gave it to him along with the crockpot.

"Thank you, I will look at your card. You know, I used to go to church. Do you think God uses the hard times to teach us things?"

"I know He does," I said.

Then he said, "My 13-year-old son has friends who are a bad influence on him."

"You need to get involved in a church so that he will meet some nice friends," I replied. "Do you go to church?"

"No," he responded, looking very guilty.

"Your boy will learn by example, won't he?"

He said, "I prayed this morning, 'Lord, there must be more to this life'."

"He heard your prayer, didn't He?"

"Yes, He did."

I told him about the Friday night youth group at our church and that the details were on the internet. He said he'd look it up. He told me that since moving into a bad area where old people were being mugged and robbed, he'd been holding meetings to talk about what the neighbourhood could do about it. He'd even asked a member of Parliament to come along.

"Do you read the Bible? It's all in there," I said.

"I'll have to get back to it, won't I?" he said, and I prayed that he would.

Healing a blind puppy

Our son Trevor and his wife Wendy were going on holiday and asked if we could look after their six, 5-week-old Alsatian pedigree puppies. We said yes and were shown what we needed to do to look after them. There was one which cried all the time. I studied this little ball of fluff and decided it was blind as it would follow the wall rather than go across the room to the other puppies. My sister-in-law Joan was visiting and I showed the pup to her. She agreed it was blind, which was sad because they would probably have to put it down.

Then one day I thought, "What am I doing? My God is able to heal the eyes of this pup." So I placed my hand over its eyes and commanded them to be healed in the name of Jesus and thanked Jesus for hearing my prayer. I then put the puppy down on the floor and saw it run over to the other puppies, no more crying. Jesus has given us His authority, His anointing and all we have to do is to ask and He does the rest. "And I will do whatever you ask in my name, so that the Father may be glorified in the Son" (John 14:13).

EPILOGUE

Something to Celebrate

On my 60th birthday I was woken by Howard and told to have breakfast, get dressed and pack some warm gear as I was being picked up at 8:30 a.m. Unbeknown to me, the family had arranged for me to go skydiving at Mercer. When we arrived, with my head under a coat so I couldn't see the signs as we approached, I was asked to get out of the car. When the coat came off, all was revealed – how exciting! Years ago when we were living in Nelson I had asked Howard if I could go skydiving. At that time his reply was: "I think I have suffered enough!" Poor dear, he had been through a lot with this wife of his. I thought then that I would never be able to parachute so put it out of my mind but here I was.

What a day! Four of our grandchildren were there to watch their nana, along with one of the mothers and a cousin, jump from a plane. A lovely young Christian man took me up in tandem so I was free to praise my God as I floated in pure adoration of the beauty I saw all around me. The instructor let me direct the parachute for a while, zooming left then right until we went into a cloud. I laughed the whole way down and loved every minute.

Ten years later, I flew around Auckland in a helicopter, celebrating my 70th birthday and our 50th wedding anniversary. I am so grateful to my husband and family for the fun times they have arranged for me during the years of trials. I am a spontaneous person and love to have fun. Sometimes I can get bogged down with the things happening around me and to have a family that knows this and sees an opportunity to make mum laugh is priceless. Thank you, family. "A cheerful heart is good medicine, but a crushed spirit dries up the bones" (Proverbs 17:22).

Along with the fun times, I am grateful for the lessons I have learnt during my walk with God.

God's Word, the Bible, is definitely alive; everything I need for each day is there. When I ask for help He is there to guide me. I need Jesus in my life every day. Living life in my own strength makes my day hard. Asking Him to go before me in all things makes my day light, not heavy.

I've discovered how important it is to have a friend I trust and am accountable to – someone who will speak truth to me so I can come before Jesus and ask Him to help me change. I have an unruly mouth that can hurt others. When God shows me how I have caused hurt, I ask Jesus to forgive me and then I must not hesitate to apologise and ask forgiveness. I have not mastered this lesson yet but am working on it. I ask Jesus to help me hear the truth, know the truth and speak only the truth and then the truth will set me free.

When I have been hurt by others, I immediately speak this blessing over that person: "The Lord bless you and keep you; the Lord make His face to shine upon you and be gracious to you; the Lord lift up His countenance upon you and give you peace" (Numbers 6:24-26, RSV). When you choose to bless, the hurt has been replaced by His peace and His love for that person.

Submitting my mind, will and emotions to Him each day helps keep me on an even keel. The armour of God is a must for everyday life (Ephesians 6:10-18). I am still learning to stop and ask the Holy Spirit how I should pray and what I should do and say in certain situations. He is infinitely wiser than I am. I have learnt over the years that my God is a supernatural God and I can trust Him in all circumstances. I feel I can honestly say that without Jesus in my life I would not be here today.

I have so enjoyed writing this book but before I conclude it, I would like to invite you to get to know Jesus and follow Him as I have done. Jesus sees everyone as equals. There is no class distinction with Him; he sees a murderer, pastor or a child the same. Jesus loves each one of us individually just as we are. If you're not sure how to begin, all you need to do is say this simple prayer out loud:

> *Dear Jesus, please come into my heart. Thank you for dying for me. Please forgive me for the bad and selfish things I have done in my life. Thank you for accepting me as your daughter/son. I believe I am now a new person in Christ Jesus.*

If you have prayed this prayer, I encourage you to tell someone you trust and find a Christian church close by with people who can tell you how Jesus died and came to life again and how the Holy Spirit lives within us. Ask God to guide you. To those who already love Jesus, I encourage you to listen to the Holy Spirit because He is talking to you, all day every day. Be obedient to His voice – you too can reach out to people around you, no matter what their situation. And be encouraged – we live in His strength, not our own.

www.ingramcontent.com/pod-product-compliance
Ingram Content Group UK Ltd.
Pitfield, Milton Keynes, MK11 3LW, UK
UKHW020241250726
13967UKWH00001B/495

9 780473 409999